Customer Portfolio Management

Management on the Cutting Edge series

Abbie Lundberg, series editor

Published in cooperation with *MIT Sloan Management Review*

Marco Bertini and Oded Koenigsberg, *The Ends Game: How Smart Companies Stop Selling Products and Start Delivering Value*

Christian Stadler, Julia Hautz, Kurt Matzler, and Stephan Friedrich von den Eichen, *Open Strategy: Mastering Disruption from Outside the C-Suite*

Gerald C. Kane, Rich Nanda, Anh Nguyen Phillips, and Jonathan R. Copulsky, *The Transformation Myth: Leading Your Organization through Uncertain Times*

Ron Adner, *Winning the Right Game: How to Disrupt, Defend, and Deliver in a Changing World*

Satish Nambisan and Yadong Luo, *The Digital Multinational: Navigating the New Normal in Global Business*

Ravin Jesuthasan and John W. Boudreau, *Work without Jobs: How to Reboot Your Organization's Work Operating System*

Mohan Subramaniam, *The Future of Competitive Strategy: Unleashing the Power of Data and Digital Ecosystems*

Christopher B. Bingham and Rory M. McDonald, *Productive Tensions: How Every Leader Can Tackle Innovation's Toughest Trade-Offs*

Thomas H. Davenport and Steven M. Miller, *Working with AI: Real Stories of Human-Machine Collaboration*

Ravi Sarathy, *Enterprise Strategy for Blockchain: Lessons in Disruption from Fintech, Supply Chains, and Consumer Industries*

Lynda Gratton, *Redesigning Work: How to Transform Your Organization and Make Hybrid Work for Everyone*

John Horn, *Inside the Competitor's Mindset: How to Predict Their Next Move and Position Yourself for Success*

Elizabeth J. Altman, David Kiron, Jeff Schwartz, and Robin Jones, *Workforce Ecosystems: Reaching Strategic Goals with People, Partners, and Technologies*

Barbara H. Wixom, Cynthia M. Beath, and Leslie Owens, *Data Is Everybody's Business: The Fundamentals of Data Monetization*

Eric Siegel, *The AI Playbook: Mastering the Rare Art of Machine Learning Deployment*

Malia C. Lazu, *From Intention to Impact: A Practical Guide to Diversity, Equity, and Inclusion*

Daniel Aronson, *The Value of Values: How Leaders Can Grow Their Businesses and Enhance Their Careers by Doing the Right Thing*

Benjamin Laker, Lebene Soga, Yemisi Bolade-Ogunfodun, and Adeyinka Adewale, *Job Crafting*

Fred Selnes and Michael D. Johnson, *Customer Portfolio Management: Creating Value with a Large Leaky Bucket of Customers*

Customer Portfolio Management

Creating Value with a Large Leaky Bucket of Customers

Fred Selnes and Michael D. Johnson

The MIT Press
Cambridge, Massachusetts
London, England

The MIT Press would like to thank the anonymous peer reviewers who provided comments on drafts of this book. The generous work of academic experts is essential for establishing the authority and quality of our publications. We acknowledge with gratitude the contributions of these otherwise uncredited readers.

This book was set in ITC Stone Serif Std and ITC Stone Sans Std by New Best-set Typesetters Ltd. Printed and bound in the United States of America.

Library of Congress Cataloging-in-Publication Data is available.

ISBN: 978-0-262-04962-7

10 9 8 7 6 5 4 3 2 1

Contents

Series Foreword   vii

1   The Value of a Large Leaky Bucket   1
2   The CPM Framework and Relationship Segments   9
3   CPM Growth   27
4   Customer Portfolio Lifetime Value   47
5   CPM Analytics   63
6   Linking CPM Strategies to Business Performance   83
7   Capturing Value through CPM   97
8   Getting Started with CPM: A Roadmap   107

Notes   115
Index   125

Series Foreword

The world does not lack for management ideas. Thousands of researchers, practitioners, and other experts produce tens of thousands of articles, books, papers, posts, and podcasts each year. But only a scant few promise to truly move the needle on practice, and fewer still dare to reach into the future of what management will become. It is this rare breed of idea—meaningful to practice, grounded in evidence, and *built for the future*—that we seek to present in this series.

Abbie Lundberg

Editor in Chief

MIT Sloan Management Review

1 The Value of a Large Leaky Bucket

Our Interest in CPM

To the executives and managers for whom this book is written, the concept of *customer portfolio management*, or CPM, is intuitive. We are hardly the first to suggest that firms can improve their financial performance by focusing on all the customers in their portfolio. Yet the business literature is replete with strategies that oversimplify the management challenge. CPM is not just about creating volume through a large customer base. Nor is it just about creating more satisfied and loyal customers. It's about how to create value with all the customers in a portfolio over time. The basic principle of CPM is to view a company's market strategies as long-term investments in the strength of relationships over an entire portfolio of current and future customers.[1] Understanding when and how much to focus on acquiring customers, defending and leveraging those relationships, and converting some of those relationships to stronger, more profitable ones are key strategy decisions for growing both the current and future value of a portfolio. The relative importance of these actions requires an understanding of a company's cost structure, its available resources, the heterogeneity of its customer needs, and the potential for customers to grow their relationship with a brand.

Our interest in CPM is rooted in our research on customer satisfaction and the creation of closer and more valuable customer relationships. But we learned some important lessons along the way. Firms have competing priorities, very different relationships with customers, and those customer relationships should be managed differently. Let's start by taking a closer look at what we learned.

The Value of Strong Relationships

One of the more universally applicable findings from marketing research in recent decades is the value of increasing customer satisfaction to create stronger, more profitable relationships with customers. As an overall evaluation of a customer's experience with a product or service provider, customer satisfaction has emerged as a key indicator of business performance and a firm's ability to capture customer revenues well into the future. The development of national customer satisfaction indices in the 1990s, including the American Customer Satisfaction Index, has led to an extensive body of both academic and applied work on the value of satisfaction toward creating stronger and more profitable relationships.[2] The research findings are clear—customer satisfaction has well-documented, positive impacts on profit per customer, overall profitability, and a firm's market value.[3]

Not surprisingly, our research, teaching, and consulting over the past thirty years has developed measurement and management systems designed to increase customer satisfaction, loyalty, and profit. That closer customer relationships are more valuable is straightforward, as a repeat customer generates more cash flow over time than a single transaction. Organizationally, however, the allure of focusing on current sales remains compelling, especially when a salesforce or management team is rewarded on short term goals. The fundamental problem with a focus on current sales is that transactions are not independent over time—not all sales are equal. In an early example of this loyalty effect, the annual profit from credit card customers was shown to be directly related to the age of a customer's account. Profit per customer is initially negative, due to the marketing costs of acquiring customers, but grows steadily with the age of the account.[4] This led to the popular metaphor that a "leaky bucket" of customers, where dissatisfied customers were constantly leaving or leaking from the bucket to be replaced by new customers, was a poor business model. The cost of constantly adding new customers to replace those who left was far greater than the cost of delivering higher satisfaction and loyalty to plug the leaks in the bucket. This led some companies to focus myopically on building a smaller, watertight bucket of loyal customers to increase profitability.

One of the authors was running an executive seminar on customer satisfaction and the loyalty effect when the discussion took an interesting turn. After explaining the virtues of improving satisfaction and loyalty, an executive from a large US telecom company was convinced that they needed to increase satisfaction and lower the annual churn or turnover in their customer base, but only by 5 percent. The other executives in the seminar were rather underwhelmed by what seemed like a modest goal in an industry where churn in customer accounts at the time exceeded 50 percent annually. The executive's response was both simple and profound. A more aggressive target would have significant, negative consequences. Only so many customers remain loyal no matter how satisfied they are. With a customer base in the millions, a more aggressive target would significantly decrease the size of the base and undermine the company's ability to employ thousands of people and keep hundreds of offices open. Put simply, they would lose economies of scale and become a smaller business with lower overall profits.

We learned another lesson from our studies of how B2B (business-to-business) firms manage their customer relationships. Pan Fish was a fish farming company that is now part of Mowi ASA, a Norwegian seafood company with over $5 billion in revenue and approximately 20 percent share of the global salmon and trout markets.[5] Pan Fish faced a particular challenge. It lacked control over its harvests, specifically the size and quality of each seafood catch. This created significant uncertainties and disruptions in the supply chain, higher costs, and unpredictable pricing. Pan Fish saw an opportunity. It grew sales and increased profits by developing different value propositions for different customer relationship segments. It sold the most preferred, medium-sized range of the catch to *partners* with whom it had developed close working relationships (i.e., industrial manufacturers of smoked salmon). It developed a customized quality control and logistic solution for these customers which brought higher margins. The bulk of smaller and larger fish were sold to *friends*, or regular customers (i.e., grocery store chains and other large retailers), and the remainder of the catch was sold in an opportunistic manner to *acquaintances* who bought primarily on price (i.e., opportunistic buyers representing hotels and restaurants). The results were a higher average profit per customer, lower operating costs, and greater overall profits. In chapter 2 we return to this typology of acquaintances, friends, and partners in more detail as a basis for *relationship segmentation*.

What did the US telecom company and the Norwegian fish farming company have in common? They were both engaged in customer portfolio management. The telecom executive understood the need to balance efforts to increase satisfaction and loyalty for some customers with the need to maintain their scale of operations by including weaker relationships in their customer portfolio. The fish farming company segmented its customers by the heterogeneity of their needs and developed value propositions for different relationship segments, from strong to weak. These examples taught us what was lacking in many business models—a framework for growth that integrates competing business priorities, the creation of more satisfaction and loyalty in customers while reducing cost per customer through economies of scale.

At its core, the CPM framework views a firm's market strategies as investments in customer relationships and projected cash flows over time. This includes entire portfolios of current and future customers involving both weaker and stronger relationships. Understanding when and how much to invest in acquiring, defending, leveraging, and growing these relationships are key business strategy decisions that affect both current and future cash flows. Depending on a company's and market's characteristics, the return on relationship investments may be maximized by having a larger number of weaker relationships in a portfolio, increasing the cash flow from a subset of closer relationships, or increasing the duration of that cash flow.

CPM builds upon perspectives in marketing, economics, and management strategy.[6] Economist Michael Porter has long emphasized the importance of incorporating both cost leadership and differentiation into a firm's strategy decisions.[7] More specifically, when should firms compete on cost and when should they compete on product or service differentiation? But balancing these different priorities is far from simple, which leads us back to the metaphor of the leaky bucket.

The Value of a Large Leaky Bucket

The *value of a large leaky bucket* illustrates both the concept and complexity of CPM. Consider the choice between two very different buckets, or portfolios, of customers: (1) a smaller, watertight bucket of loyal and profitable customers, or (2) a larger, albeit leaky bucket of customers that includes both stronger and weaker customer relationships. Our research and applications of CPM have taught us that it is typically more profitable in the long run to pursue a larger, leaky bucket. The value lies in the prospect that all customers in a portfolio have the potential to create value.

The stronger, longer-lasting relationships in a portfolio are generally more profitable. However, even the most loyal customers eventually leave a portfolio. Even travelers who are titanium customers in Marriott's Bonvoy program or platinum customers in Delta's SkyMiles program eventually reduce their travel and hotel stays. Put simply, loyalty is fleeting. Consider two other examples from our studies. A farm equipment supplier conducted a profitability analysis of its customers and identified the 5 percent who were the most profitable customers in its portfolio, labelled priority customers. The salesforce allocated significantly more of its time to these customers given their value. Two years into the process, the profitability analysis was repeated and revealed that one-third of these priority customers had fallen below the criteria for inclusion in the group based on annual sales and gross margins, while an equal number of new customers now qualified as priority. The company had not recognized that within the priority segment, customers had varying probabilities for continuing the relationship. In the second example, a cable TV supplier's most profitable customer segment was males in their late 20s living alone or sharing an apartment with a friend. These customers not only bought cable TV access but typically bought the most advanced cable TV packages and were heavy users of broadband. But they also had very high levels of churn, or turnover, based simply on the fact that they moved more frequently than others. The average duration of these customers was approximately 24 months compared to 100 months for the rest of the customer portfolio.

The lesson is that even a smaller, watertight bucket of customers "evaporates," while the value of the weaker relationships in a portfolio is twofold. Weaker relationships both increase scale, or lower cost per customer, and provide a valuable source of future loyal customers. Not all stronger customer relationships last forever and not all weaker relationships are poor investments. The value of a large leaky bucket is that it includes both stronger and weaker relationships. Even in cases where relationship conversion is very profitable, constantly adding new customers to a portfolio is an essential part of CPM. Ongoing customer acquisition drives growth and lowers costs. It recognizes that some of these new customers will be coming and going, in transactional relationships, while some have the potential to become closer, more profitable relationships. From a strategy perspective, one of the most important questions to answer is which holes in the bucket to plug, and which holes should continue to leak? The CPM framework is designed to help answer these questions.

In our applications of CPM, we have found that the use of relationship segments that include true partnerships with customers comes more naturally to B2B (business-to-business) companies than B2C (business-to-consumer) companies. In B2B settings, buyers and sellers are more aligned and likely to work closely with each other on customized solutions within supply chains to create stronger relationships. But the B2C environment is changing. Digital platforms involving companies like Amazon, Apple, and Google require greater and greater end-user adaptation to a brand's systems and processes. Then there is IKEA, the international furniture retailer that has built a successful strategy around developing partnerships with both suppliers and end users.[8] IKEA customers adapt significantly to IKEA's systems and processes as they research what to purchase online and in catalogues, drive long distances to stores, navigate and explore large retail spaces, pick furniture out of a warehouse, and then drive home and assemble the furniture themselves with instructions based completely on pictures. The result is a greater overall value for customers and a competitive advantage for IKEA with respect to cost and efficiency. Another example is the development of brand communities. Brands including Harley-Davidson, Lego, Jeep, and even Taylor Swift offer opportunities for customers to actively participate with other members of a brand community in events and experiences that build brand relationships.

The lesson is that whether in a B2B or B2C context, the more customers and brands learn from, collaborate with, and adapt to each other, the stronger and more valuable the relationships and the greater the likelihood that a partnership emerges. Still, relatively few firms work systematically to optimize the value of their customer portfolios. Even firms that excel at relationship development will underperform when they fail to understand market dynamics and how value is created across an entire portfolio of customer relationships. Whether a firm offers goods, services, or integrated solutions, we offer valuable lessons for executives and managers who seek to grow their customer portfolios and profits.

Chapter Organization and Takeaways

The chapters that follow are designed to give the reader an overview of the CPM framework, its strategies and prescriptions, and the analytics and models that drive implementation. Chapter 2 introduces the three major building blocks of the framework: (1) segmenting brand relationships into strangers, acquaintances, friends, and partners; (2) understanding customer portfolio lifetime value; and (3) making the key management decisions that follow, namely customer acquisition, relationship defense, relationship leverage, and relationship conversion. Chapter 3 focuses on CPM growth strategies. We use Amazon, Apple, and IKEA as examples of companies that successfully manage their customer portfolios and use differentiation and customization to create strong, profitable brand relationships. Other examples are used to illustrate the application of acquisition, conversion, defense, and leverage strategies to each of the different relationship segments. The concept and modeling of *customer portfolio lifetime value* is the subject of chapter 4, which includes prescriptive strategies that underscore the importance of balancing both offensive and defensive marketing strategies. When, for example, should the emphasis be on volume and scale, as through weaker relationships, and when should greater emphasis be placed on creating closer customer relationships? And what strategy makes sense in markets where turbulence in the form of cost or price shocks are more frequent?

Subsequent chapters focus on the how-to of CPM. Chapter 5 delves into CPM analytics, including database principles and the importance of descriptive statistics, causal inferences, and predictive scoring analytics. Chapter 6 reviews customer satisfaction modeling and highlights the information needed to drive the quality improvements and innovation related to customer acquisition, retention, and relationship conversion. We end with two discussions. Chapter 7 raises the question, "what is marketing management anyway?" We argue that marketing management has become a dynamic process focused on mapping a portfolio of products and brands into a portfolio of customer relationships. Chapter 8 reviews the basics of CPM and provides tips on how to jump-start the process, as through a focus on digitalization. This includes how firms should balance people, processes, and technology to advance their CPM strategy.

Our audience includes the business executives and managers responsible for increasing the lifetime value of one or more customer portfolios, as well as the industry consultants and academics who support them. Students interested in a broader framework for making customer-centric business decisions will also find our approach useful. Our goal is to leave the reader with a framework that balances competing business priorities, most importantly the scale economies derived from current sales versus the lifetime value of loyal customers. CPM is not about taking a singular or myopic focus on loyal customers or an obsession with scale. Rather, it is about understanding the value of a large leaky bucket of customers, one that balances both priorities. In the chapters that follow we introduce ideas for growing the value of a customer portfolio and explore the impact of digitalization and brand communities on CPM strategies. We trust that you will find the journey both interesting and valuable.

2 The CPM Framework and Relationship Segments

Building Blocks

The framework of CPM involves three major steps or building blocks: (1) *relationship segmentation*, (2) *customer portfolio lifetime value* (CPLV), and (3) the management decisions that follow (see figure 2.1). The process begins with the segmentation of customers into four relationship-based populations: strangers, acquaintances, friends, and partners. CPLV is about understanding the expected revenues and costs over time across relationship segments. The management decisions required to increase the value of a portfolio include the importance of *customer acquisition, relationship defense, relationship leverage,* and *relationship conversion.*

In traditional market segmentation, unique populations of customers are segmented and targeted using differentiated products and services. The segments are based on differences in customer needs, wants, or benefits sought, be it a soup that is thicker and tastier or a bank that is friendlier. A cornerstone of marketing management for decades, needs-based segmentation remains an extremely valuable approach and embedded within CPM.[1] The limitation of traditional needs-based segmentation, however, is its focus on a particular product or service category and brand. It is a relatively static approach that presumes customers are in a particular needs-based segment. The reality is that customer behavior is dynamic, where a company's or brand's customers are active in multiple needs-based segments within and across product or service categories. Customers use a portfolio of brands that evolves over time and depends on the context or usage occasion. A Marriott Bonvoy customer may, for example, book more self-service brands such as Residence Inn or Fairfield Suites early in their relationship

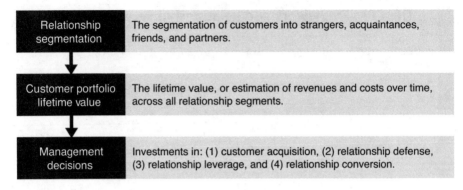

Relationship segmentation	The segmentation of customers into strangers, acquaintances, friends, and partners.
Customer portfolio lifetime value	The lifetime value, or estimation of revenues and costs over time, across all relationship segments.
Management decisions	Investments in: (1) customer acquisition, (2) relationship defense, (3) relationship leverage, and (4) relationship conversion.

Figure 2.1
The framework of CPM.

and migrate to more luxury brands such as Ritz Carlton or J. W. Marriott over time. At any given point in time they may seek an upscale or distinctive brand for special occasions or business travel while preferring select service brands when traveling with their kid's sports team. A banking customer may look to the bank with the lowest interest rate and best payment terms when they need a loan, migrate to a bank with better wealth management services as they accumulate savings, or use more than one bank at the same time for different needs.

In our applications of CPM, we have found that the best place to start is to segment customers based on the strength of their relationship with a brand. As in the case of Pan Fish, the fish farming company from chapter 1, what typically emerges are three distinct segments of existing customers, *acquaintances*, *friends*, and *partners*, where each segment seeks a different value proposition based on different needs. We have found that these segments are robust across industries and applications. That said, these segments only capture the customers who are already in a portfolio. One needs to add *strangers*, which includes prospective future customers and those who have switched to a competitor or otherwise left a portfolio, in order to complete the segmentation scheme. Strangers include both true strangers and customers who are essentially estranged.

The second building block of CPM is understanding how the concept of *customer lifetime value* (CLV) applies across the relationship segments in a portfolio, which we refer to as customer portfolio lifetime value. Traditional measures of CLV estimate the expected future revenue or profit from a given customer over the course of their relationship with a company or brand.[2] CPLV is the lifetime value of an entire portfolio of relationship segments.[3] Unlike estimates of CLV, the broader consideration of CPLV takes important additional considerations into account. CPLV places value on the strangers who have yet to enter the portfolio or have left but have the prospect of returning. Highly valued consumer brands such as Nike or Starbucks may lose customers temporarily but have a significant probability of gaining them back in the future in what may be a relatively strong albeit not continuous relationship. Thus, investments in building brands yield future revenues within CPLV. CPLV also incorporates the value of product and service categories where customers have yet to (but are likely to) purchase in addition to what they are currently buying. This is the principle of relationship leverage where, for example, a bank customer with a history of everyday banking has a higher probability of becoming a life insurance or mortgage customer than a noncustomer. A third difference is that CPLV incorporates the notion of shared costs over and above marketing costs. When new customers are added to a portfolio, they pick up a share of the fixed costs, which increases the margins on existing customers. These differences represent portfolio-level benefits that are not captured in CLV models.

We use different but complementary approaches to estimating CPLV in our research and applications. Our academic research operationalizes CPLV as a prescriptive model.[4] The model includes a large set of variables related to unit costs, customer acquisition, switching behavior, and conversion from weaker to stronger relationships. It estimates cash flows from different relationship segments based on different market conditions to forecast revenues and costs over the course of one or more product life cycles. We explore this model in detail in chapter 4. The value of this approach is that it illustrates how different market conditions impact CPLV, showing how different customer segments contribute to both current and future cash flow. As the CPLV model involves a large set of variables and estimation well into the future, it is difficult to operationalize in practice, although companies can use similar, pro forma–type models to simulate cost, price premiums, and revenues under different scenarios over time.

We use a different approach to estimating CPLV when applying the framework in the context of a specific company or brand. Here we use a combination of relationship segmentation and existing customer lifetime valuation methods. We work with management to identify a practical

approach to segmenting an existing customer portfolio into different relationship segments. We then use CLV-type calculations at the relationship-
segment level as the basis for calculating overall CPLV across segments.
Later in the chapter we provide an example of this approach in a retail
context. The disadvantage is that this approach does not consider the population dynamics mentioned, including estranged customers who return
to a strong brand, downstream cross-selling opportunities, or shared costs.
Thus, we have found a combination of CPLV modeling and case applications to complement each other as we gain a better understanding of CPM.

The third building block of our framework includes the management
decisions that are core to CPM. In our work with executives and managers
across multiple industries, these decisions boil down to four key questions
and resulting goals:[5]

1. Which customers to target, including specific investments in customer
   acquisition.

2. How to protect the portfolio from defections or churn, recognizing that
   there are many different strategies for defending relationships.

3. How to leverage the relationships created, such as through more frequent
   purchases, higher volume purchases, or cross-selling bundled products
   and services.

4. How to convert weaker relationships into stronger, more profitable relationships, again recognizing that there are different strategies to do so.

Resources devoted to customer acquisition are tied closely to the desired
scale of operations and resulting unit costs. Innovation and continuous
improvements that increase satisfaction and loyalty are keys to both relationship defense and relationship conversion. Relationship leverage, as
through more frequent purchases, higher volume, and cross-selling or bundling products and services takes advantage of the lower marketing costs
associated with stronger customer relationships. And the value of relationship conversion, that is the conversion of weaker relationships into stronger ones, depends on both customer heterogeneity and competition. Brand
differentiation ultimately depends on the existence of very different needs-
based segments, a brand's adaptation to those needs, and whether competitors can easily follow and compete for the same segments.

The CPM framework builds upon a large body of research on, and applications of, *customer relationship management* (CRM). A basic tenet of CRM

is that understanding the exchange relationship between buyers and sellers is central to understanding the role of marketing in an organization.[6] This research demonstrates how exchange relationships develop, expand, and dissolve in predictable ways, where some relationships are contractual, some discrete, and others more relational.[7] Moving from discrete or transactional exchanges to true relationships requires a level of commitment and trust that engenders closer cooperation between buyers and sellers.[8] A relational view of marketing is credited with putting the customer first and shifting a narrative that was focused on sales to one based on genuine interaction and knowledge-sharing with customers.

As we noted earlier, relationship development has received particular focus in a B2B or industrial marketing context.[9] Industrial buyers and sellers become more dependent on each other, or locked into a relationship, through various investments that include physical assets, delivery systems, cooperative pricing arrangements, and exclusive dealerships.[10] In our salmon farming example, Pan Fish invested in a customized logistics system for its salmon smoking customers who, in turn, invested in manufacturing equipment tailored to the size of the salmon. The commitments that buyers and sellers make in these relationships, some of which are unique to the relationship, provide both benefits and act as powerful signals of commitment.[11] At the same time, these investments and commitments create switching costs where buyers and sellers may become "hostages" in the relationship.[12]

The CPM framework developed here provides a holistic yet practical approach to relationship management. Whereas traditional approaches typically lump friends and partners together, the differences are real, and we have found that these relationships should be managed differently. In a similar vein, the business strategy literature generally distinguishes between differentiation and cost leadership strategies. However, friends and partners require very different levels of differentiation, while cost leadership depends on all the relationships in a portfolio. This brings us to step one in the framework, our typology of relationship segments.

Relationship Segments and Segmentation

CPM starts with relationship segments and segmentation, where the segments are based on the principle that customers form very different

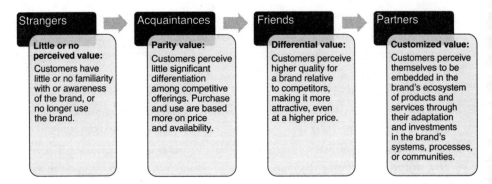

Figure 2.2
Value propositions by relationship segment.

relationships with individual brands, companies, or organizations. We refer to the sellers in these relationships simply as "brands" and the customers or end-user consumers simply as "customers." Figure 2.2 describes our relationship typology where customers are segmented as strangers, acquaintances, friends, or partners. Each relationship in the typology is described using its unique brand-based value proposition.[13] The flow from weaker to stronger relationships captures the concepts of customer acquisition (from strangers to acquaintances) and relationship conversion (from acquaintances to friends and friends to partners).

True strangers either have no familiarity with a brand or limited familiarity, such as through advertising, word of mouth, or previous trials. We also include estranged (former) customers in this segment, recognizing that a value proposition exists for these customers but has either become weaker than competitors or no longer fills a need. Strangers do not include all noncustomers, but rather target customers who have the potential to become customers or reengage with the brand. They may be new to the market, earlier customers who have not returned, or customers who have an ongoing relationship with competing brands. The strategy for acquiring new-to-the-market customers follows a traditional marketing management process of creating awareness, trial, and repeat. The strategy for acquiring customers from competing brands is different depending on the strength of the relationships. Convincing another brand's customers to switch likely requires more time, effort, resources, and customer insight the closer the relationship customers have with the competing brand.

Acquaintances are familiar with the brand from a purchase or use stand-point and find it equally attractive to, or on par with, competitors. This parity value means that purchase and use are based primarily on price, availability, and familiarity. Customers buy relative commodities, such as energy or many food products, from whatever brand is most convenient and has the lowest price. Notice that this type of acquaintance value may be found in such categories as vehicles, clothes, restaurants, and wherever a proportion of customers perceive that available alternative brands have more or less the same value proposition. Acquaintances are likely to return or stick with a brand simply because their familiarity creates less uncertainty. Friends have a stronger connection with the brand, perceiving it to be different and better than other brands in one way or another. Their satisfaction is higher, and they repurchase and use the product or service even at a higher price given a stronger overall value proposition. Partners, in contrast, feel a more direct and personalized connection to the brand, where the brand "knows" them and together they create a more attractive and customized solution space in an ongoing relationship where satisfaction is even higher. As noted, Apple and Amazon customers both adapt to and benefit from the brands' systems, processes, and communities, which create greater value propositions for customers. This adaptation helps turn friends into partners, which increases their propensity to stay with the brand and expand their relationship into new product and service categories. An important point is that a typical brand will have customers in all segments—strangers, acquaintances, friends, and partners—where customers evolve from one type of relationship to another over time.

In the framework of CPM, acquaintances provide both a source of future loyal customers and a basis for scale economies, while friends and partners provide greater margins and future cash flows. Stronger relationships increase customer expectations, brand preference, usage, and resulting customer satisfaction. As satisfaction and relationship strength grow, so does a customer's willingness to share knowledge and adapt to a brand's systems, services, and brand extensions, thus increasing margins and lowering costs per customer.

Relationship segmentation is the identification of unique populations of customers based on the nature of their relationship with a brand. Even in the absence of more sophisticated analysis, a better understanding of which customers are in which relationship segments goes a long way toward improving the management of a portfolio. Our relationship typology of strangers, acquaintances, friends, and partners resonates strongly with practitioners and has a strong basis in research. Naturally, some portfolios have more relationship levels, and some have less, depending on the nature of the business and heterogeneity of demand. Yet the classification of an existing customer base into acquaintances, friends, and partners is a robust approach. In business research, exchange relationships have been found to vary from discrete transactions or encounters to pseudo-relationships to true interpersonal relationships.[14] These distinctions share important features with our typology. Encounters are just that, encounters or an individual transaction. Pseudo relationships occur when customers are repeat buyers who may interact with different individuals each time, although service providers have access to information about customers (such as through CRM systems or loyalty programs). True interpersonal relationships occur when a customer has repeated contact with the same individuals in a firm, where customers perceive and experience a personal connection with the service provider.

The main point of departure with respect to our typology is that we focus on customer relationships with a brand, company, or organization, not just personal relationships with individual service providers.[15] Our typology incorporates the strength of a brand's value proposition—parity value, differential value, or customized value—as fundamental to relationship conversion and competitive advantage. Recall that strangers become acquaintances when their awareness and interest lead them to try the brand, where repeat purchases are more dependent on price, availability, or familiarity. Acquaintances evolve into friendships when customers receive a differentiated offering that generates both higher satisfaction and a level of trust in the relationship. As the flow of information between the brand and the customer increases, that information is disseminated throughout an organization to produce improved products and services. Converting friends to partners requires an even higher level of perceived value, information sharing, and customers' willingness to adapt to a brand's systems, processes, and communities. Brand offerings become more customized, leading to even higher levels of relationship commitment.

The Segmentation Process and Lifetime Value

Categorizing customers into relationship segments is the result of a segmentation process. There are a variety of approaches to sorting existing customers into acquaintances, friends, and partners. We recommend using a combination of measures that include customer preference, satisfaction, purchase volume, and gross margins to classify customers into segments. Later in the chapter we provide an application of CPM to a building materials retailer where measures of brand preference and share of wallet are used to identify relationship segments. The resulting segmentation scheme included acquaintances with greater than 50 percent share of wallet, acquaintances with less than 50 percent share of wallet, friends who preferred the brand with less than 50 percent share of wallet, and partners who preferred the brand with more than 50 percent share of wallet. The segments emerged from a dialogue with management to ensure they were meaningful to the retailer. They also capture the fact that the retailer's portfolio included high volume acquaintances.

Loyalty programs are another basis for relationship segmentation, as with Marriott's Bonvoy program or Delta Air Lines' SkyMiles program. Based on points earned for hotel stays and related purchases, Bonvoy customers earn up to five levels of elite status, Silver Elite, Gold Elite, Platinum Elite, Titanium Elite, and Ambassador Elite.[16] Similarly, SkyMiles customers are identified by their Silver, Gold, Platinum, or Diamond status.[17] Recognize, however, that there are important limitations when using loyalty program levels to segment customer relationships. As the segments may be based on purchase volume, higher level customers may include both high volume acquaintances and true friends or partners. The number of levels in these loyalty programs also likely map into fewer relationship segments, namely acquaintances, friends, and partners.[18]

In many B2B settings, we have found that individuals inside a company are so familiar with individual customers and their purchase histories that they can reliably classify customers as acquaintances, friends, or partners. This was the case for Pan Fish, the salmon and trout farming company from chapter 1. The labels may differ, as some firms label customers as level 1, 2, and 3, or A, B, and C, but the meaning is the same. In the case of parts suppliers in the auto industry, for example, we have observed that level 1 customers work closely with the supplier and share information to develop and provide highly customized parts, services, and delivery systems in large volume (partners). Level 2 customers are companies that regularly purchase a volume of more standardized products out of inventory (friends); and level 3 customers buy products on occasion, such as from the company's catalogue or website (acquaintances).

Another general approach to relationship segmentation is to derive segments through statistical methods. A study of telecom customers provides a good example.[19] The study used survey measures of overall satisfaction and *switching costs* (the perceived economic costs of switching brands) along with measures of actual *prior churn* (frequency of switching behavior over the four months leading up to the survey) to predict *future churn* (frequency of switching behavior over the nine months following the survey). As expected, increased levels of both satisfaction and switching costs decreased subsequent churn. The largest single predictor of future churn was prior churn. Put simply, the biggest predictor of future behavior was past behavior, where some customers are inherently more prone to switching than others.

This observation led to one of the more interesting findings, which was a significant *interaction* involving prior churn and customer satisfaction when predicting future churn. Interactions occur when the impact of one variable on another variable is, in part, dependent on the value of a third variable. Here, the impact of satisfaction on future churn was dependent on the overall level of prior churn. For customers who were less frequent switchers before the survey, customer satisfaction had a significantly greater impact on retention after the survey. For customers who were more frequent switchers, customer satisfaction had a lower impact on retention. The analysis thus revealed very different relationship segments based on customers' predisposition to churn and level of satisfaction. The implication for portfolio management is that efforts to increase customer satisfaction are better targeted toward customers who are more predisposed to stay loyal to a brand.

B2C Partnerships through Brand Communities

An important element of the value proposition for partners includes the customer's inclusion in a brand community, especially in the B2C space. Management theories and models naturally view "the firm" as the central focus. But that's not how customers view their relationship with a brand. Brand communities involve a "structured set of social relations among the admirers of a brand," where the central focus is the social network.[20] Simple brand communities, where customers interact in person or electronically with other customers of the brand, are certainly part of being an acquaintance or friend. A deeper and more dynamic view of brand communities is relevant to partnerships, where customers interact with the product or service, the brand itself, other customers in the community, or the agents of the brand.[21]

Tesla, for example, has very active online brand communities. There are Tesla Owner Clubs with local brands in the US and other countries. The Tesla Owners Club of Norway operates independent of Tesla. As with other brand forums, the main activities include the sharing of practical information regarding vehicle usage, service, software upgrades, and so forth. The forum is open to visitors (e.g., strangers) and members pay a fee to receive membership benefits. The independence of the brand community means that customers have created a power base they can use to affect the brand and how it operates. This means that Tesla must work with the clubs and cannot necessarily control negative word of mouth.

Long before Tesla owners, there were the Harley HOGs. Harley-Davidson motorcycles have long enjoyed, and actively built, a strong community of owners through its Harley Owners Group and local chapters around the world.[22] HOG members enjoy the ability to interact with other members, participate in rallies and competitions, receive newsletters, purchase merchandise, and even receive roadside assistance. Adaptation through the customization of the motorcycle itself creates a particularly unique link between the physical product and the individual.[23] Through their brand community and active participation in product customization, Harley owners form a deep loyalty to the brand. The problem Harley faces is rooted in our earlier discussion of the value of a large leaky bucket. Harley's customer base has very few leaks, but it is evaporating as it ages and registrations decline.[24] The inability of initiatives to bring new customers into the brand community has resulted in a smaller albeit watertight bucket of loyal customers. Left unchanged, declining cash flows will follow.

With independent online brand communities, companies have less control over negative word of mouth and risk severe effects on both existing customers as well as the potential for recruiting new customers. Jeep, for example, has enjoyed a longstanding and close relationship with Jeep owners. Yet Jeep clubs have recently needed to distance themselves from events that turn drunk and disorderly, and unfortunately, the brand remains associated with such events.[25] A more positive customer-driven trend has been tagged "Duck, Duck, Jeep," where Jeep owners reward and recognize fellow

Jeep owners by placing a little rubber duck on an owner's Jeep.[26] What these brand communities do provide is a way to build partnerships with customers. They are an important way in which customers embed themselves into a brand's systems and processes.

On a related note, the emergence of brand ambassadors and influencers stands to help brands build relationships at multiple levels. Brand ambassadors represent and advertise a brand or company either online or offline. These ambassadors leverage their expertise and existing social presence (e.g., public figures) to embody or personify a brand's identity. While they operate differently from formal brand communities, they help form public perceptions, provide a human touch and a degree of honesty, and can help mitigate bad reviews.[27] Brand ambassadors can help strangers to become acquaintances by inducing trial, help acquaintances become friends by communicating differentiation, or help friends become partners by engaging them in a broader ecosystem of offerings or brand community.

Customer Trajectories and Heterogeneity

In our relationship typology, we assume that some but not all strangers become acquaintances, some but not all acquaintances become friends, and some but not all friends become partners. The reality, of course, is more complex. Customers lapse in their purchases, retreat back to lower level relationships, switch to and from competitors, and even skip levels in the progression. This complexity is grounded in a process view of customer–brand relationships and resulting relationship trajectories, which vary from life-long relationships to relationships that come and go to passing flings.[28] Understanding the trajectories for acquaintances, friends, and partners will be particularly important when estimating the value of relationship segments.

Along the course of these trajectories, customers navigate a variety of tensions that help keep them on a particular trajectory or cause them to alter their relationship with a brand.[29] A favored brand could suffer a significant lapse in performance. If that lapse is addressed particularly well, their loyalty may be reinforced. If handled poorly, the customer typically has options to consider. If competitors come out with more innovative options, customers may have cause to alter their brand trajectory. The practical problem is that the development and implementation of market strategies for all possible customer trajectories quickly becomes unmanagable. In our operationalization of CPLV, we find it more pragmatic to focus on the natural progression of relationships from strangers to acquaintances to friends and, ultimately, to partners, recognizing that some customers switch to and from competitors at any given relationship level.

Understanding relationship trajectories is core to estimating the lifetime value of relationship segments. Our recommendation is to start by building simple models and frameworks to estimate future cash flows and profitability lest the approach become unmanageable. The complexity of the estimates can increase over time. A simple model for estimating future cash flow for a relationship segment, for example, is to make it a function of observed relationship volume, revenue generation, and predicted length of the relationships. If Marriott's Bonvoy system estimates that Gold, Silver, or Platinum customers book a predictable number of nights per year, at a predictable average room rate, and remain at that level over a predictable period of time, lifetime value estimates and comparisons follow.

As customer information systems grow and become more sophisticated, so does the ability to increase the complexity of the estimates. That is, relationship trajectories become more predictable. In financial services and retailing, for example, we find positive S-shaped patterns in the relationship trajectory and resulting cash flow. The probability of continuing the relationship is quite low at the start of the relationship but grows exponentially until it plateaus. In markets where customers' initial investments are higher, such as professional services or home security systems, the probability of continuity starts at a higher level and grows from there. Several variables affect both the growth pattern and the level where the cash flows level off, which correlate positively with time and other variables. It is important, however, to pick a finite period to estimate lifetime value. As we have stated, even the strongest relationships in a portfolio eventually weaken and end.

In addition to understanding relationship trajectories, the value of the typology rests on understanding the heterogeneity of customer needs, as it is heterogeneity that creates the opportunities for relationship conversion. Put simply, how much do customers, or segments of customers, vary in their underlying needs and wants? It is important to recognize two major sources of this heterogeneity: those which evolve in a market over time, and the more categorical differences in needs and wants from market to market. In any given product or service category, as customers gain experience and develop category- and brand-level knowledge, they come to appreciate differences between competing brands. This knowledge is fueled by the introduction of new and more differentiated brands.[30] As customers are inherently different, they come to appreciate different attributes, features, and underlying benefits of different brands and sub-brands. This is a common pattern in consumer-packaged goods where, over time, soap products add a variety of fragrances, cereal brands add different flavors and forms, and coffee brands add different roasts (blonde, medium, dark) and sources (fair trade, organic).

There are also category-level differences in heterogeneity, where some product or service categories are more limited in the possible range of customer needs than others. Technology and government regulation are contributing factors. The market for cellular network services and the market for mobile phones have, for example, developed very differently. Mobile network services are more a function of the latest regulated technology, such as 5G service, where differentiation is based more on area coverage and pricing. There is greater potential for differentiation among the mobile devices that operate in these networks, based on operating system (e.g., iOS, Android, etc.), size, flip, memory, camera quality, app stores, and a variety of other features.

These forms of heterogeneity beg questions related to relationship segmentation. Can a brand's ability to differentiate itself from competitors be captured in the analysis of a customer portfolio? Can a company capture friends and partners from a competitor based on a superior value proposition and differentiation? As markets mature, brands must keep up with competitors as they innovate, improve, and offer sources of differentiation. In the lodging market, for example, companies like Airbnb made great strides by providing a real alternative to traditional hotel rooms. As the lodging market has continued to evolve, however, the cost advantages of Airbnb have dwindled (as fees are passed along directly to customer), customers experience varying quality (versus the brand standards of companies like Hilton and Marriott), and the hotel brands have developed both branded alternatives (e.g., Homes & Villas by Marriott) and stronger loyalty programs. Brands that do not keep up with meeting the needs of a heterogeneous customer base provide competitors with significant opportunities to steal dissatisfied customers. Going back to our Tesla example, the brand stole friends and partners from other luxury brands like BMW, Mercedes, and Audi, because those brands were slow to provide electric vehicles with sophisticated digital functions.

A Retail Application of CPM

A CPM analysis for a European retail brand of building materials illustrates how one company used relationship segments to identify strategies for portfolio growth. The first source of data was a survey of a representative sample of the population of customers who had bought building materials from this brand during the previous two years. These customers were asked if they perceived the brand to be better than, equally good as, or worse than the competing brands they were familiar with. Next, customers were asked to provide an estimate of the share of wallet from this brand relative to other brands. Customers also indicated their total purchase volume, perceived strengths and weaknesses of the brand, and loyalty intentions.

Discussions with the management team zeroed in on customer preference and share of wallet to define four types of customers:

1. Partners who are 20 percent of customers and who perceive the brand to be both better than competitors and purchase more than 50 percent of their share of wallet from the brand.
2. Friends who are 6 percent of customers and who perceive the brand to be better than competing brands but purchase less than 50 percent of their share of wallet from the brand.
3. High volume acquaintances who are 18 percent of customers and who rate the brand as equal to or worse than other brands yet purchase more than 50 percent of their share of wallet from the brand.
4. Low volume acquaintances who are 56 percent of customers and who rate the brand as equal to or worse than other brands and purchase less than 50 percent of their share of wallet from the brand.

The first insight from the analysis is that the majority of relationships in the portfolio are weak (74 percent), with most of those relationships at a low volume. The second insight came from estimating the lifetime value of the average customer in each of these segments.[31] The expected cash flow from a partner (€3,144) was over six times the value of an acquaintance with less than 50 percent share of wallet (€466) and over one and a half times the cash flow from an acquaintance with more than 50 percent share of wallet (€1,847). The expected cash flow from a partner was also three times greater than that from a friend (€1,054). Given the percentage of customers in each segment, partners account for 45 percent of the total value of all customers but only 20 percent of the portfolio. Our analysis revealed that if acquaintances and friends developed into partners, it would increase the overall value of the brand's portfolio by 122 percent.

The most important finding for the retailer boiled down to differences across retail locations. They found a very strong connection between relationship strength and individual store performance. Stores with more friends and partners performed significantly better than those with more acquaintances. However, the strength of customer relationships varied widely across the 29 stores in the chain. Although the stores had identical product assortment and store layout and followed the same marketing programs, their relationship strength varied considerably. Figure 2.3 shows the percentage of friends and partners ranked from the highest to lowest performing store. For the best performing store (Store A), 78 percent of their customers were friends or partners, whereas the weakest performing store (Store AD) had just 13 percent. The explanation for these differences

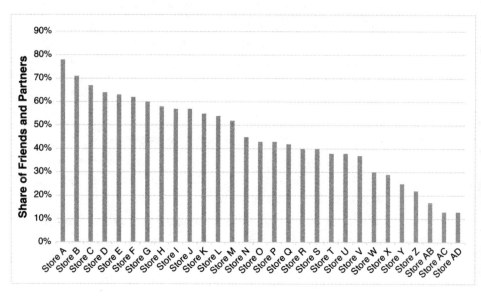

Figure 2.3
Share of friends and partners across stores.

was that both local management and local competition varied considerably from store to store. Some store managers were better able to deliver and exceed customer expectations, while in some markets competitors were better able to fulfill and exceed customers' expectations instead.

This information provided the management team with powerful facts and set the retailer in a new direction regarding its growth strategy. First, members of the team knew which stores had the highest potential for growth through relationship conversion. Second, they developed more diagnostic information about which specific elements in their offerings were important to customers, yet underperforming. (We delve into more detail regarding this diagnostic information when we discuss satisfaction modeling in chapter 6.) A weakness in service culture was identified as an important competitive vulnerability in the analysis. Third, management was able to borrow best practices from more effective store managers. The management team developed a dynamic and detailed monitoring system for its customer portfolio collecting data from different data sources including transaction data, loyalty program data, CRM data, and customer surveys. This, in turn, helped the retailer to identify key performance indicators, provided strategic direction for store managers, and improve overall performance.

Chapter Summary

Customer portfolio management balances the need to build markets in the short term by converting strangers into acquaintances with the longer-term value of turning acquaintances into friends and friends into partners. The framework of CPM rests on three key building blocks: relationship segmentation, customer portfolio lifetime value, and the management decisions that impact portfolio growth and profitability. The most important takeaway from the framework is that segmenting customers into strangers, acquaintances, friends, and partners is a robust approach to market segmentation. It effectively categorizes customers based on the strength of a brand's value proposition. The creation of partners in business-to-business relationships is well established, less so the management of an entire portfolio of weaker to stronger relationships for profitable growth. Partnerships in business-to-consumer markets, meanwhile, are growing as customers adapt to digital platforms and engage in brand communities, recognizing that platforms and communities may require very different management.

As our retail application shows, application of the framework has the potential to turn the complexity of CPM into straightforward and manageable opportunities for growth, in this case the borrowing of best practices from stores with stronger and more profitable relationships and applying them to less profitable locations. The value of building stronger versus weaker relationships rests heavily on the heterogeneity of customer needs, meaning just how much customer needs and wants vary from category to category or market to market and how they evolve over time. Our modeling of CPLV in chapter 4 explores the impact of heterogeneity on CPM strategies. Before doing so, chapter 3 takes a closer look at three companies that have built strong customer portfolios—Amazon, Apple, and IKEA—and specific strategies and examples related to customer acquisition, relationship defense, relationship leverage, and relationship conversion.

3   CPM Growth

Increasing the value of a customer portfolio involves the four basic CPM growth strategies introduced in chapter 2. The first is which new or lost customers to target with specific investments in customer acquisition. The second is how to protect the portfolio from churn, recognizing that there are different strategies for defending different relationships. Third, how the firm can leverage the relationships created, as through more frequent purchases, higher volume purchases, value-added services, or cross-selling bundled products and services. Finally, what investments should be made in converting weaker relationships into stronger, more profitable relationships, again recognizing that there are different strategies for doing so.

Customer acquisition grows the size of the portfolio and resulting economies of scale, while recognizing that some relationships are fleeting. Acquisition strategies keep adding water to the leaky bucket. *Relationship defense* is the process of using customer information systems to identify and fix "things gone wrong" to minimize customer defections. This plugs those holes in the leaky bucket that should be plugged. *Relationship leverage* takes advantage of lower marketing costs among closer customer relationships to grow sales through frequency of use, share of wallet, and additional product and service offerings. And *relationship conversion* is the process of improving "things gone right," through differentiation and customization, to create closer customer relationships. The more customers are acquired, retained, and converted to stronger relationships, the more the business will grow, be profitable, and increase shareholder value. This requires offering products and services that customers find more attractive than competitors' offerings, which brings about higher expectations, making them more challenging to deliver. The reward, however, is sustainable growth of the customer portfolio.

CPM requires an understanding of both what customers want in a relationship with a brand and their propensity to either engage in a stronger relationship or remain at arm's length. Call it customer focus, customer centricity, or customer insight, the point is that companies use their understanding of customers to create relationships and defend those relationships from competitors. In situations where the number of customers is relatively small, this insight may be gathered through personal interaction and direct communication with customers. When the number of customers grows to the thousands or millions, it requires a customer database and measurement system that is predictive and facilitates the management of a complex ecosystem of buyer–seller relationships.

CPM at Amazon.com

Amazon is an excellent case study of a firm that effectively manages a large, global population of customers through its digital platforms, data analysis, and self-described obsession with customers. Here we examine Amazon's customer insight and digital marketing strategy through the lens of CPM. Amazon's systems include both transactional measures that facilitate the design of better service processes and models that link actions to customer behavior and retention. Amazon's success is deeply rooted in its obsession with customers. As founder and former CEO Jeff Bezos states:

> We seek to be Earth's most customer-centric company and believe that our guiding principle of customer obsession is one of our greatest strengths. . . . By focusing obsessively on customers, we are internally driven to improve our services, add benefits and features, invent new products, lower prices, increase product selection, and speed up shipping times—before we have to.[1]

The quote provides two important insights. Being customer-centric is viewed as a strong competitive advantage at Amazon, where the value proposition in its B2C channel is based on providing a wide variety of products and services that are easy to use, at low prices, delivered fast and free, with excellent customer service. The quote further emphasizes the importance of using customer insight to drive internal product and process change through innovation and continuous improvement, and to do so before the competition.

Amazon's digital marketing strategy has been described as a four-step process of reach, act, convert, and engage.[2] Amazon reaches out to prospective customers using SEO (search engine optimization) and targeting millions of advertising keywords. Easy-to-use online experiences, such as the ability to "look inside" potential book purchases or read product reviews entice customers to act—that is, to make a purchase. Personalized recommendations and a best-in-class checkout process helps to create loyal, repeat purchasers, some of whom adapt even further to Amazon's systems and processes by purchasing across product categories and providing recommendations of their own to other customers.

Conceptually, there is nothing fundamentally new about this approach. It employs tried-and-true frameworks that encompass both offensive and defensive marketing strategies. The early stages of a customer's adoption of a product or service involve awareness-trial-repeat (ATR).[3] Product diffusion models (models that predict sales and market share over the course of a product's life cycle) have long relied on the notion that unless a brand creates awareness, there will be little trial, and without satisfactory trial, there will be limited repeat purchases. Similar approaches to sales funnel management have involved creating customer awareness, interest, decisions, and actions.[4] Once a customer has developed a relationship with a brand, predictive or propensity modeling helps companies to link quality, customer satisfaction, and loyalty and understand their impact on business performance.[5]

There is also a tremendous amount that is new in Amazon's applications. It uses customer data from digital platforms and sophisticated data analytics that include AI and machine learning on a large scale to inform marketing decisions.[6] The resulting strategy reflects an organization that effectively manages millions of customers on an individual level. When customers lapse, or don't purchase for a while, individualized reminder ads and specials are sure to follow. When customers search and are indecisive, their search history is used to remind them of something they may want to reconsider.

While much has been written about Amazon, its success has not been examined within the framework of CPM. One quickly observes how Amazon excels at all four key management decisions in the framework:

Customer Acquisition: Amazon constantly attracts new customers to its portfolio with over 300 million customers in over 100 countries.[7] As its growth accelerated, the number of customer accounts was growing 20 percent annually, giving Amazon tremendous scale relative to competitors.[8]

Relationship Conversion: Amazon has successfully converted over 200 million of these customers to Amazon Prime membership worldwide.[9] Prime member benefits include free shipping, video streaming, deals, music, and more, while the Prime shopping app has become one of the most popular retailer apps in the US.

Relationship Leverage: Amazon encourages customers to invest in the brand's array of products and services, resulting in higher brand value for the customer and both current and future cash flow for the brand. It leverages relationships through broader brand usage and adaptation, extensions into new product categories, lower unit costs, lower margins on high volume items, and higher margins on lower volume items. Amazon has been very successful in extending its brand into a diversified and interconnected offering. It started with books, but now customers can purchase electronics, clothing, shoes, sporting goods, jewelry, home and kitchen products, and much more. Amazon thus generates a greater share of wallet from its customers at a lower cost per customer.

Relationship Defense: Amazon retains customers by fulfilling expectations, creating satisfied customers, and building trust. Amazon has historically high customer satisfaction scores among online retailers, and it never rests on its success.[10] Rather, it continuously innovates around its offerings, online ordering, and delivery systems to defend and protect the relationships in its portfolio.

Amazon's success in managing a large customer portfolio has resulted in exponential growth and $575 billion in annual sales in 2023.[11]

Differentiation at Apple and IKEA

Because customer relationships vary with respect to future cash flows and responsiveness to offerings, companies must differentiate or customize those offerings to compete for those cash flows. This includes the differentiation or customization of product offerings, service processes, and customer programs. Product differentiation and customization are about what physical qualities, specifications, or features to offer different relationship segments at what price. Service differentiation is about what service processes to offer different relationships at what price. That may include expedited wait lines, delivery systems, upgrade options, or dedicated help lines for loyal customers—think airline or hotel loyalty programs. Program differentiation is about developing unique programs or activities designed to help convert customers from one relationship level to another, such as membership in a brand community. But offering the wrong product specifications, service process, or program to the wrong relationship segment will result in a poor allocation of resources.

Both Apple and IKEA have built strong customer portfolios and sustainable growth through different forms of differentiation and customization. Building customer relationships at Apple has involved a combination of products, services, and programs, but it did not happen overnight. In 2001, Apple launched its iPod as an easy-to-use mp3 player. At that time, competing mp3 players were complicated to use and adoption rates were low. The iPod simplified the process of downloading music onto a device and its advertising campaigns fostered an image of being "hip." In 2003, Apple opened the only legal digital catalog for major record labels, the iTunes Store, allowing customers to buy albums or individual songs.[12] It elevated expectations for the category, exceeded expectations for users, and built a strong and positive brand attitude. In 2007, Apple introduced the iPhone as an app-based, easy, and fun-to-use mobile telephone and a new era of growth followed. Apple has continued to set and meet high expectations, growing its portfolio of valuable and loyal customers through a larger and larger ecosystem of products and services. On the service side, this now includes iCloud data storage and Apple TV+ streaming services. From a program and brand community standpoint, Today at Apple offers "free sessions at your local Apple Store and online to get hands-on with the latest from Apple."[13] These devices, services, and programs represent but a portion of Apple's offerings. The more customers adapt to the system, the less likely they are to switch to competitors.

IKEA is another brand that illustrates the principles of customer portfolio growth. It is a story that spans the better part of a century.[14] Ingvar Kamprad founded IKEA back in 1943 at the age of 17. He slowly but surely built a strong competitive advantage through a company culture based on thrift, inventiveness, and hard work, known as the IKEA Way. Furniture entered the product line in 1948, after which IKEA began selling mail-order furniture at factory prices far below competitors to help young families with little income to establish their first home. Competitors threatened IKEA's suppliers with boycotts, but IKEA's popularity and orders continued to grow. Necessity was the mother of invention at IKEA as Kamprad turned problems into opportunities, brought design and production in-house, created "knock-down" packaging to lower costs, and expanded outside of his native Sweden for production to provide affordable designs and home furnishings for the many people who have fewer resources.

Over time, IKEA has built a network of linked activities involving its well-designed products, service processes that directly involve the customer, and programs that adapt to customer needs. This saves both the company and the customer money. IKEA's services include kitchen planning, delivery, and partnerships with companies like TaskRabbit for customers who want help assembling the furniture.[15] With respect to programs, IKEA has responded to customer concerns regarding sustainability. The company is on track to meet its 2030 climate commitments, and its accomplishments include 100 percent renewable energy use in all IKEA-owned factories, 99 percent of the wood used in products being FSC (Forest Stewardship Council) certified or recycled, and creative ways to care for IKEA products (refurbishment, buy-back options, spare parts).[16] As its product, service, and program mix has grown, IKEA had not only grown its customer base but developed closer partnerships with both customers and suppliers through the unique culture of IKEA and sales continue to grow.

But let us focus specifically on the four CPM strategies related to customer acquisition, relationship defense, relationship leverage, and relationship conversion. The logic of growth within the framework of CPM is laid out in figure 3.1, where CPM strategies build brand relationships, and stronger brand relationships grow the size of a portfolio, relationship duration, and cash flow per segment. We start with the first and fourth

Figure 3.1
CPM strategies and portfolio growth.

strategies, customer acquisition and relationship conversion, as they represent different portions of the overall process of relationship development. We then explore, in turn, relationship defense and relationship leverage.

Customer Acquisition and Relationship Conversion

Customer Acquisition

Put simply, customer acquisition is about establishing or reestablishing an exchange relationship with a brand. Recall that strangers are not *all possible* strangers, but rather those in a brand's target market. Target customers involve those who are both new to the market and those who have an ongoing relationship with other brands, making for very different acquisition strategies. Most product and service markets follow a life cycle, or diffusion pattern, where customers enter the market at different points in time. Growth early in a life cycle is slow and based primarily on customers who are innovators or early adopters. When the market reaches an inflection point where demand takes off, customers enter the market at an increasing rate. Growth eventually levels off, resulting in an S-shaped diffusion curve.

This growth pattern applies to stand-alone product or service categories as well as successive generations of technology, such as cell phones and cell phone service. As strategies for customer acquisition are well developed in marketing management and strategy, we do not cover them in detail here. Simply stated, they involve a thorough understanding of customer needs; the fit of a new product or service to customer needs that are not being met; and the investments in advertising, distribution, and positive word of mouth required to create brand awareness, trial, and repeat customers. This is traditional market segmentation, positioning, and brand management.

Acquiring customers from competing brands is a different story, where acquisition depends on the strength of the customer's existing relationship with another brand. If the customer is a competitor's acquaintance, the competitor may enjoy little or no perceived differentiation. Consider target customers for Amazon's Kindle app and e-books who still buy hard copies in bookstores based on price and convenience. Amazon's strategy would be to offer an even lower price, greater convenience, and easier information search. Target customers for the opening of a new IKEA store would include customers who buy from traditional furniture stores but see IKEA as offering comparable quality at lower prices.

In addition to offering lower cost, convenience, or both, opportunities arise when competitors' customers are dissatisfied with their offerings. Dissatisfaction creates opportunities often exploited in customer acquisition strategies, such as with the success of Altibox, a Norwegian cable and broadband company. Its customer acquisition strategy has rested on creating higher customer satisfaction than competitors and using that to capture competitors' customers when contracts are up for renewal. In the transition from cable to broadband, targeted customers switched to Altibox because of their dissatisfaction with previous suppliers. From 2018 to 2021, Altibox customer satisfaction continued to improve while competitors' satisfaction continued to decline.[17] Significant increases in market share for Altibox followed.

When target customers are friends of competing brands, it means that they perceive significant differentiation. Customers have chosen the competing brand because they perceived it to be better on one or more product or service qualities. Here it is necessary to convince target customers that your brand offers differentiation beyond availability and familiarity. The motivation to switch is a value proposition that is a noticeable improvement from their ongoing relationship with a competitor. A classic example is Nike's 1987 introduction of the Nike Air Max running shoes. Friends of competing brands including Reebok, Adidas, Puma, and Brooks were attracted to the unique cushioning technology offered by Nike's new shoe, driving an increase in market share. Continued advances in running shoe technology have helped Nike maintain its hold on a large segment of runners over time.[18]

Whereas Nike used product innovation to attract competitors' customers, service firms use other types of process and image innovations to create similar results. Scottish Widows, a life insurance and pension brand, used an innovative advertising concept to create awareness and trust in a highly competitive market and attract new customers. The narrative from the company's origins in 1815 was that of a mutual life office that delivered security for widows, sisters, and other female relatives so they would not be plunged into poverty on the passing of the fundholder during and after the Napoleonic Wars. The modern icon portrays the Scottish Widow as a character who confronts any negative associations with the word "widow" through the values of strength, reliability, integrity, innovation, and heritage. As noted on the company's website, "Our current Widow, Amber

Martinez is seen as contemporary, confident, someone who's there watching over and providing support to our customers at key points during their lives."[19] The campaign categorically increased brand awareness, trust, and switching behavior from competitors.

Converting Acquaintances to Friends

As in the case of acquiring customers from competitors, converting acquaintances to friends is about creating an advantage that goes beyond price, convenience, or buying habits. The brand must develop a value proposition that connects with customers' underlying needs. Consider an automotive dealership that found that 50 percent of acquaintance customers were households with two or more vehicles, where most customers purchased those vehicles from different dealerships. The dealership developed a "carpool" concept where customers would receive value-added services and discounts if they bought more than one vehicle from the dealer. These value-added services included pick-up service when a vehicle was in for maintenance and a free rental vehicle in case of engine failures. With the new value proposition, they converted many of their acquaintances to friends.

When converting acquaintances to friends, it is important to have a deep understanding of the heterogeneity of customer needs. Remember that needs-based segmentation doesn't go away in the framework of CPM. Rather, it becomes a dynamic process where any given relationship segment includes customers with different, albeit overlapping, needs-based segments that evolve over time. While two acquaintances may have become customers based on equivalent needs, their conversion to friends may be rooted in different needs. For example, new mortgage customers often become customers based on an attractive interest rate. But their interest in additional products from the bank (be it investments, insurance, pension plans, etc.) may be rooted in very different preferences and needs. One customer may be converted based on financial acumen and reputation, another on the convenience of bundling both products with the same supplier. Thus, in converting acquaintances to friends, companies need to be sensitive to underlying differences in customer needs.

Converting Friends to Partners

Converting friends to partners is about motivating customers to adapt even further in their relationship with a brand to enhance their value proposition. The result is a stronger defense against competing brands, reduced costs, and a solid foundation for extending the brand into new product and service categories. As noted, partnering is well established in B2B markets where suppliers and customers coordinate and make specific investments in their relationships. In the earlier case of Pan Fish, the Norwegian fish farming company, those investments were with smoked salmon producers who needed a customized product and service supply chain. Successful partnerships are a win-win for both parties: a greater value proposition for customers, and higher prices, lower costs, or both for the supplier or brand. For the supplier, cost reductions may appear in production, logistics, customer service, or sales. For the customer, benefits accrue in the form of lower operating costs, better products and services, and lower search costs. Whereas partnering is traditionally thought of as a B2B concept, the evolution of information technologies and digital platforms works as an accelerator in creating partnerships in consumer markets as well.

Partnering is different from built-to-order customization because this form of customization does not require any form of adaptation to shared resources or activities. Built-to-order vehicle purchases are, for example, more about searching for and selecting a vehicle based on make, model, body style, size, engine (gas, hybrid, or EV), exterior color, and so forth. Partnering is more about developing customized solutions based on shared information, shared activities, and relationship-specific investments, such as the customized logistics solution that Pan Fish provides its partner customers or the active participation of suppliers and customers in IKEA's business model. It is about creating a different level of interaction between buyers and sellers. The most powerful consequence of the ongoing digitalization in the car industry is less about customization of the product (built-to-order or mass-customization) and more about the impact of digitalization toward embedding customers in the brand's ecosystem of products, services, digital systems, and brand communities.

Starbucks, for example, has successfully converted friends to partners through the preorder process and loyalty program linked to its mobile app. This allows customers to place an order on their way to the coffee shop and avoid having to wait in line. While customers save time and enjoy their coffee sooner, Starbucks lowers costs through better capacity utilization and productivity. The digitalized interaction creates great learning opportunities for both the customer and brand. The app links customers to relevant information including product sourcing, processing, and new products. Starbucks uses the information to better understand customer preferences and behaviors to target emails and promotions, identify new locations, and guide product development.

Apps with recommendation systems, such as Amazon and Spotify, offer another avenue for digitalization to foster partnerships. As Spotify's system usage increases, customers are more likely to provide feedback that enables the system to make music, playlist, and other entertainment recommendations. Spotify customers save time in searching for new music they may like. Sophisticated users adapt and learn how the algorithms work and use that knowledge to train the recommendation systems to improve performance. Based on these idiosyncratic investments, switching barriers increase.

Digitalizing interactions with customers will continue to evolve and create opportunities for differentiation and customization. Ontex, "a leading international personal hygiene group, has developed a smart solution to improve incontinence care for patients" that has led to steady growth.[20] Its smart diaper improves the wellbeing of patients, professional caregivers, institutions, and families using smart sensors linked to a phone app to optimize the cost associated with continence care. The nature of the relationship between the Ontex brand and its institutional customers has changed from being a provider of products to becoming a solution provider offering both products and services.

Relationship Defense

Strategies for defending relationships—that is, limiting defections or churn—vary across strangers, acquaintances, friends, and partners. And there are important differences between contractual and noncontractual relationships. In contractual relationships, customers commit to paying for a product or service over a period of time, be it subscriptions to newspapers, fitness centers, cellular plans, or streaming services. Time-based contracts may also apply to insurance policies, mortgages or loans, and housing rentals or leases. The focus in these relationships is on contract renewal, often referred to as churn management, where the timing of potential churn is more predictable. In noncontractual relationships, the timing is far less predictable. Remember, an important lesson of the large leaky bucket metaphor is that loyalty is fleeting. Loyal airline, hotel, restaurant, or retail customers will at some point decide to stop using the brand or to use the brand less frequently. In these cases, loyalty program data and changes in purchase and usage patterns help predict whether a customer will remain active and loyal.

Defending Strangers

Strangers are an important source of new customers where the principal strategy is to preserve what brand familiarity and interest exists. Promotional strategies and other forms of marketing communication help secure a brand's level of future consideration and inclusion in potential customers' evoked sets of brands. Even with little or no familiarity, strangers maintain some awareness of the brand as an option when entering a market as first-time customers. OneCall, a Norwegian mobile services brand, has been very successful in building a high level of brand awareness and interest relative to its market share.[21] By investing heavily in advertising and creative concepts, potential customers see OneCall as a smart, friendly alternative to bigger brands in the market.

Defending Acquaintances

Acquaintances are familiar with a brand through purchase and usage but see little in the way of differentiation beyond price and convenience. Churn or defections in this case are likely due to lower-than-expected quality, perceived cost relative to other brands, or simply the emergence of a better option whose attractiveness exceeds any switching costs. The customer satisfaction measurement and management systems described in chapter 6 are designed to reduce "things gone wrong" across product and service qualities and maintain customer satisfaction. They also present opportunities to deepen a relationship with customers by improving "things gone right."

Consider the case of Sector Alarm, a leading provider of safety alarm systems, which has grown its customer portfolio to include over 600,000 satisfied, loyal customers across Europe.[22] But early in its growth, Sector Alarm experienced a significant and unexpected decrease in satisfaction and increase in churn. When customers called customer service they were frequently put on hold, and when they got through to a person, frontline employees had a poor understanding of the problem and possible solutions to remedy the situation. Customer dissatisfaction was high and defections increased. Taking a close look at its customer feedback, the data showed that the defections were directly related to systems that were experiencing false alarms. A deeper analysis of the false alarms revealed that the alarm systems were very dependent on changing batteries. When battery power was low, the system sent messages to the household that something was wrong with the system, and when customers called customer service, they provided little help. As the problem escalated, customers became frustrated, even furious, and began contacting competitors.

Sector Alarm turned the problem into an opportunity. The company used its customer knowledge to communicate the issue throughout the organization, improve the alarm systems, and align incentives from sales to service. It not only improved product issues that were draining the batteries but developed a system to monitor battery age. It offered customers bundled services that included adding an automated system to notify customers two to three months in advance that the battery needed changing, as well as the option of a battery monitoring and replacement service. As a result, it ended up creating closer, more profitable customer relationships.

Defending Friends

As friends choose a brand based on perceived attractiveness beyond cost or convenience, leaving the relationship is based on a failure of the brand to provide clear differentiation, a competitor's ability to exceed that differentiation, or significant changes in the cost or convenience of competitive offerings. Put simply, has the customer's motivations to switch to a competitor come to exceed the reasons to stay? As friends and partners expect more from a brand, their reasons to stay or switch may be very different. In chapter 6 we focus on the customer measurement and quality improvement decisions that both give customers reasons to stay and remove reasons to leave. As noted earlier, in the language of quality management, these are typically referred to as improving "things gone right" and removing "things gone wrong." It becomes important to understand how these drivers of customer satisfaction and retention vary across relationship segments.

Defending friendships is a common problem for educational institutions. In the US, for example, approximately one-third of all college students transfer to another institution before earning their degree, typically after their freshman year.[23] The friendship created upon entering college is lost or never progresses into a partnership. A European business school identified the lack of connections that students form with the institution as a primary contributor to this churn. The school found that the number of students leaving after one year was close to 25 percent, representing a large financial loss for the school and a loss for students who leave before finishing their degree. Three factors contributed to their leaving. The rigor of the curriculum exceeded the ability of some of the students who were admitted; students lacked conviction that they had chosen the right bachelor program; and some failed to create social connections with other students. To limit churn, the school put more resources into developing students' ability to succeed in the curriculum, provided counseling to motivate students to continue, and created more opportunities for new students to connect with classmates during their first year. Over time, churn decreased, and the school developed longer-lasting relationships with more students and a deeper understanding of their needs.

Defending Partners
Partners actively invest in and adapt their buying behavior in their relationship with a brand, expecting greater benefits, lower costs, or both in return. The brand is expected to reciprocate and show good will, reflecting its own commitment to the relationship. They will, of course, experience episodes, like when the coffee shop coffee is cold or the airline flight is cancelled. Customers, understanding that failures occur or things go wrong, expect redress for the failure to the best of the brand's ability. Brand adaptation, as core to a partnership, suggests that customers will not only update their transactional expectations but also their relationship expectations. Thus, reasons for leaving a partnership include failures to provide high transactional utility (a hot coffee or an on-time flight), failure to provide relational expectations (a free coffee or an airline seat upgrade as redress), or both. Given the level of adaptation and relationship-specific investments in a partnership, customer switching costs also factor greatly into the motivation to switch to another brand.

Relationship Leverage

Relationship leveraging also differs in contractual and noncontractual relationships. In contractual relationships, the cross-selling of additional products and services may occur within the contracting process. When purchasing a new vehicle, for example, dealerships cross-sell as many additional product and service packages as they can, from extended warranties to service maintenance packages, which provide predictable cash flows downstream. For noncontractual relationships, customer information systems help identify potential cross-selling opportunities (e.g., a recent search or inquiry), and cross-selling promotions follow.

Leveraging Acquaintances

Upon creating acquaintances, fitness centers are quick to promote add-on services. SATS is a leading provider of fitness and training with over 270 clubs across the Nordic countries. Interested customers are offered tailored solutions to increase their engagement.[24] These tailored solutions include branded concepts that address individual fitness needs, including physiotherapy, childcare, and saunas. Retailers like IKEA use displays and promotions to increase sales-per-visit. New IKEA customers, after navigating the myriad of showrooms, typically purchase more items than they anticipated. Tying customer acquisition to entry into a brand's customer club or loyalty program, like at large US retailers like Costco or REI, immediately establishes a digital communication channel and opportunities for digital promotions. The emergence of these channels provides several benefits, including lower media costs, promotions that address specific customer needs, and better data for analyzing the return on promotional spending. Customers benefit by having more control over the promotions they would like to receive.

Leveraging Friends

Leveraging friendships requires a deeper understanding of customers' belonging to a relationship segment and segment needs. TUI fly Nordic is part of the TUI Group, a large German leisure, travel, and tourism company. For many years TUI fly Nordic promoted its vacation properties in Europe to families traveling with small children. Peak seasons were school holidays, and in offseasons it promoted its hotels largely through heavy price discounts. A closer examination of its customer portfolio revealed a segment of older friendships, typically couples 50 and older, who deliberately avoided peak seasons. Interviews with these customers revealed that they preferred to travel in the offseason because there were fewer children using the amenities, making for a more relaxing environment. TUI fly Nordic also found that these older customers booked more expensive hotels, spent more money in the hotel restaurants, and often bundled transportation (airline) services through the same company. TUI fly Nordic realized it had wasted an opportunity by discounting offseason tickets. It redesigned its promotional activities, bundling strategies, and pricing to address both families with children and couples 50 and older, aimed at different vacation windows, with an immediate increase in cash flow from its older customers. Put simply, it stopped giving away rooms to customers who enjoyed off-peak visits.

Leveraging Partners

One of the best ways to leverage (and defend) partner relationships is to continuously enhance the customer experience or reduce customers' costs where products and service offerings are interlinked. The principle is that the more a customer becomes embedded in a brand's ecosystem of products and services, the more value they obtain. This embedding may be technology-driven, for example, that which happens with personal computers and connected devices. The Apple ecosystem mentioned earlier has only grown over the years to include desktop computers, laptops, iPads, iPhones, smart TV, smartwatches, AirTags, payment services, iCloud storage, and more. Amazon's ecosystem has grown to include Twitch, Amazon Web Services, Amazon Music, Audible, Whole Foods Market, and more. Both companies motivate customers' continued adaptation and investment in the brand relationship, thus increasing cash flows from customers. In addition to what the brands offer directly, they support brand communities, or customer-to-customer relationships. As partnering gains momentum, it reduces marketing costs and increases economies of scale, effectively combining Michael Porter's cost leadership and differentiation strategies.

A CPM Guide to Strategies and Action Steps

What emerges from these examples is a guide to the strategies and action steps of CPM. Figure 3.2 captures these strategies, where the rows in the matrix represent the management decisions of CPM (customer acquisition, defense, leverage, and conversion) and the columns represent the relationship segments (strangers, acquaintances, friends, and partners). The matrix prioritizes points of emphasis in your CPM strategy whether, for example, the focus is on customer acquisition, defense, or conversion (and leverage).

	Strangers	Acquaintances	Friends	Partners
Acquisition	**Create awareness:** Create and build brand awareness, familiarity, and positive word of mouth.	**Create parity value:** Induce trial (or reestablish prior relationship) through promotion of the price and availability of products and services to target customers.	**Create differential value:** Develop and communicate more attractive brand value propositions of product and service offerings that are moreattractive, even at a higher price.	**Create customized value:** Work directly with customers to share knowledge, innovate, and create a customized brand offering.
Defense (Retention)	Maintain brand awareness, familiarity, and positive word of mouth among noncustomers.	Remove "things gone wrong" (reasons to defect). Offer loyalty program awards to induce repeat purchases, reward purchases, and create switching costs.	Improve "things gone right" and loyalty program benefits (reasons to stay) to maintain differentiation vis-à-vis competitors. Increase satisfaction and switching costs.	Innovate with customers to embed them further in a brand's ecosystem. Deliver high customer satisfaction and higher switching costs.
Leverage	Encourage noncustomers to share their brand awareness with others.	Use price promotions and loyalty program incentives to induce purchase of additional products and services.	Leverage the lower marketing costs among friends to extend the relationship to additional product and service categories.	Continue to leverage customer knowledge sharing and lower marketing costs to grow the ecosystem.
Conversion (Relationship Progression)	**Convert strangers to acquaintances:** Induce trial (or reestablish purchasing) through promotion of the price, familiarity, or availability of the brand to target customers.	**Convert acquaintances to friends:** Educate customers regarding the benefits of differentiation, where brand communities and ambassadors may play a role.	**Convert friends to partners:** Educate customers regarding the benefits of customization and a closer partnership within a brand's ecosystem or product and service offerings, where brand communities and ambassadors may again play a role.	**Sunset partners:** When loyal customers eventually reduce or discontinue their purchases, continue to give the relationship the respect it has earned and deserves. Create brand ambassadors for life!

Figure 3.2
Strategies and action steps.

Acquisition strategies focus on creating awareness and trial early in a relationship, where parity value is the main goal. Product and service differentiation and customization are the keys to acquiring friends or partners respectively.

Relationship defense, or retention, builds on elements of quality improvement, a topic we turn to in more detail in chapter 6. The retention of acquaintances is focused primarily on removing "things gone wrong" or the basic qualities that the product or service should provide. Retaining friends focuses more on improving "things gone right," that is the performance attributes that provide differentiation, while defending partners is an ongoing process of innovation through customer collaboration and knowledge sharing. Relationship leverage, meanwhile, ranges from the use of price promotions and loyalty programs to increase the volume of purchases for acquaintance to leveraging the lower marketing costs associated with closer customer relationships to bring customers further and further into a brand's ecosystem of product and service offerings. Finally, conversion strategies are a process of inducing trial and educating customers as they move from weaker to stronger brand value propositions, where the brand communities and ambassadors introduced in chapter 2 may play a role.

Two cells in the matrix fill missing links in our discussion. The first addresses what it means to leverage strangers. One simple idea here is to encourage noncustomers to share positive brand awareness—knowledge and word of mouth—with other strangers. Brand communities often include strangers who aspire to be customers (e.g., prospective Tesla owners or Harley HOGs). These knowledgeable strangers could be encouraged to share their knowledge and experiences with other strangers. The other interesting cell involves the conversion of partners as a relationship declines. We call this *sunsetting* partners. The issue here is that, for one reason or another, the customer trajectory is coming to a natural decline or endpoint. The objective is to retain the goodwill that these customers still embody. Consider the business traveler who spent years accumulating miles and loyalty benefits on an airline, then moves toward retirement and travels less frequently, but still travels. One of the authors has accumulated close to 2 million miles on one airline. He still flies that airline whenever he can, receives upgrades albeit less often, and its CRM system recognizes him as a million miler. His patronage may not mean as much as it used to, but the acknowledgement of past patronage and loyalty and the respect it conveys pays dividends in other ways. Properly sunsetting customer relationships has the potential to create brand ambassadors for life.

Chapter Summary

Our CPM framework and applications over the past two decades underscores a fundamental principle: "It's in a company's best interest to view its market strategy as a long-term investment in the strength of relationships over an entire portfolio of current and future customers."[25] Amazon has accomplished this principle on a large scale, while brands including Apple and IKEA have used a combination of products, services, and programs to continually differentiate themselves and create strong customer relationships. Our takeaway from discussions with managers and executives engaged in CPM is to break down the management decisions into four key goals and strategies: customer acquisition, relationship defense, relationship leverage, and relationship conversion. Brands from Nike to Scottish Widows use product differentiation and creative positioning to acquire new customers. Sector Alarm, faced with customer defections, used product improvement and value-added services to turn a problem into an opportunity to defend relationships. Tui fly Nordic leveraged its relationship with older customers to offer a better off-peak vacation experience, while Amazon leverages it customer relationships through cross-selling a larger and larger digital platform of products and services. And Pan Fish used a customized solution to convert friends into partners.

With these and earlier examples in mind, in chapter 4 we turn to understanding the concept and modeling of customer portfolio lifetime value (CPLV). While building upon earlier concepts and strategies like CLV, CPLV is different. Using our metaphor of the value of a large leaky bucket, CPLV balances the need for sales volume, economies of scale, and lower costs with the value of creating stronger, more profitable relationships with customers.

4 Customer Portfolio Lifetime Value

The CPLV Model

In the years following World War II, economies of scale and scope were central to business and offensive marketing strategies prevailed. As competition increased and markets matured, the lifetime value of customers became a priority, giving rise to more defensive strategies. Recall that the primary aim of offensive marketing is to increase the size of one's customer base, as through increased market share or market size, whereas the primary aim of defensive marketing is to retain existing customers, as through customer satisfaction, switching costs, or both.[1] Along the way, the global economy has been rocked by such events as the bursting of the dot-com bubble, the COVID-19 pandemic, and various banking crises and global conflicts. The reality is that markets are inherently dynamic and in perpetual motion. As new generations of technology and related life cycles emerge, priorities shift from offense to defense, back to offense, with varying levels of shocks in the system. From a CPM perspective, both offensive and defensive marketing are ongoing processes that contribute to CPLV.

Our modeling of CPLV takes these strategies into account through the inclusion of both scale economies and customer heterogeneity. Our earlier discussion of the value of a large leaky bucket makes it clear that economies of scale and scope, and learning curve effects, are essential strategy considerations. In addition to scale and scope, however, customer heterogeneity is an essential characteristic of markets. Customer heterogeneity recognizes that customers have very different needs and prefer different brand-value propositions. The more heterogeneous the customer needs, the more firms respond by differentiating and customizing their offerings. The more differentiated and customized the offerings, the more customers are willing to problem solve and invest their time and effort in brands to obtain greater value. These dynamics move acquaintances to become friends, and friends to become partners. And as market offerings become more differentiated and customized, customers are more satisfied, with higher switching costs, and more loyal behavior.[2]

The implication is that, as customer heterogeneity increases, companies and brands stand to gain more from recognizing and managing all the relationships in a customer portfolio. In this chapter we introduce our model of customer portfolio lifetime value (CPLV) to illustrate the effect of scale economies and customer heterogeneity on the dynamics of a portfolio, where customers convert from strangers to acquaintances, acquaintances to friends, and friends to partners. We then describe how additional financial value is created when companies invest disproportionately (relative to competition) in strategies focused on acquiring new customers, defending customer relationships, or converting weaker relationships to stronger ones. We describe how brand extension strategies are more valuable in heterogenous markets and, finally, how relationship investments help shield companies against market shocks.

The Constructed Market

The CPLV model was developed to help us understand how portfolio management, the existence of scale economies, and customer heterogeneity influence market dynamics and cash flows over time.[3] Recall that CPLV is the lifetime value of an entire portfolio of exchange relationships. The value extracted from these exchanges depends on both the customer and the brand. While our earlier work demonstrates the positive impact of scale economies on CPLV, more recent simulations described here focus on the impact of customer heterogeneity under different scenarios.

Our extension of the CPLV model specifies several parameters as follows:

- The model runs over 120 periods (e.g., months).
- The model involves two competing brands, our focal Brand A and a competing Brand B, the latter of which may represent a class of competing brands.
- The number of new customers entering the market follows a traditional S-shaped diffusion curve. Upon entering the market, customers continue to purchase one brand or the other every market period.

- In each period customers can either continue their relationship with the same brand or switch to the competitor.
- The degree of customer heterogeneity in the market is captured by monthly retention and conversion rates. In low heterogeneity conditions, customer retention rates from period to period are set to 80 percent for acquaintances, 81 percent for friends, and 82 percent for partners. In high heterogeneity conditions, these retention rates are set to 80 percent, 83 percent, and 85 percent, respectively. Thus, when customer demand is more heterogeneous, customer retention rates increase. Relationship conversion rates in low heterogeneity conditions were set to 0.1 percent for acquaintances to friends and 0.2 percent for friends to partners. In high heterogeneity conditions these conversions rates increase to 2.0 percent and 3.0 percent.

Figure 4.1 illustrates the relationship structure of a portfolio in conditions of low versus high customer heterogeneity (e.g., relative commodities versus differentiated offerings). The vertical axes represent the number of customers in the portfolio by relationship segment. The horizonal axes represent the market period (from 0 to 120). When customer demand is more homogeneous (low heterogeneity), acquaintances dominate the portfolio. As heterogeneity increases, more customers convert to stronger relationships and retention rates grow. Here we observe that acquaintances dominate the portfolio in the early stages of market development while friends and partners become the larger relationship segments over time.

The cash flow from these customer populations in the CPLV model is computed as the *contribution margin*, or revenues less costs, of each customer relationship segment multiplied by the number of customers in each relationship segment in a market period. Each segment differs with respect to prices paid and costs incurred. We define these revenue and cost parameters as follows:

- The baseline unit price that acquaintances pay is set to $100 and kept constant.
- As customers convert from acquaintance to friends and friends to partners, they pay price premiums of 20 percent over the baseline price, making the price $100 for acquaintances, $120 for friends, and $140 for partners. These price premiums are based on a greater willingness to pay for differentiated and customized brand value propositions for friends and partners.

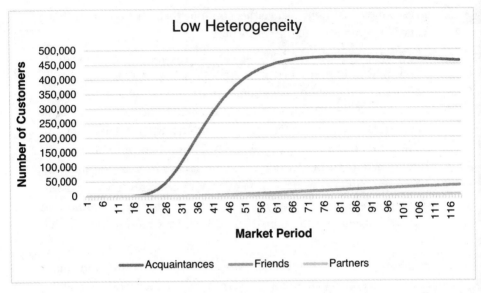

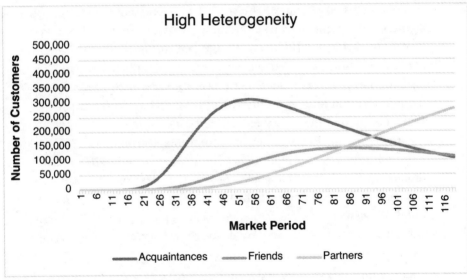

Figure 4.1
Customers over time in low versus high customer heterogeneity conditions.

- Unit cost is set to $70 in the first period and economies of scale defined to approach 50 percent of the initial unit cost ($35) with accumulated production.

- For partners, the unit cost is further reduced by 10 percent due to the customers being embedded in a brand's ecosystem, which reduces marketing costs and makes transaction activities more efficient.

- The cost of acquiring a new customer is set to $5, while the cost of acquiring an acquaintance, friend, or partner from a competitor is set higher to $50, $75, and $100.

- The costs associated with retaining customers (defensive marketing activities) are set to $20, $5, and $2 for acquaintances, friends, and partners respectively given increasing levels of satisfaction and switching costs as relationships grow.

- The cost of converting an acquaintance to a friend and converting a friend to a partner is set to $50 and $75, respectively.

- The response functions for investments in acquisition and retention is S-shaped, meaning that a minor increase (relative to competition) will have an initial, marginally increasing effect followed by a marginally decreasing effect on acquisition and retention.

- The response function for conversion investments is exponentially positive meaning that increased investment in conversion activities will have exponentially larger effects on conversion.

Using these parameters to compute customer portfolio cash flows requires several steps. The cash flow from acquaintances is a function of the number of acquaintances and their contribution margins. The number of acquaintances in a market period is the sum of acquaintances retained from the previous period, converted first-time customers, and acquaintances acquired from competitors, less the number of customers either converted to friends or lost to competitors. The contribution margin for acquaintances is the baseline price minus the unit cost and market activity costs. The computation of cash flow from friends and partners follows the same logic with different price premiums for friends and partners—with the unit cost reduction (through efficiency) for partners.

As market conditions change, the cash flows from acquaintances, friends, and partners develop very differently. In our simulations of CPLV, we have found that firms operating in a market with more homogeneous customer demand (low heterogeneity) accumulate approximately 40 percent less cash flow than those operating in markets with relatively heterogeneous demand. This argument is consistent with those of industrial economists like Michael Porter who argue that companies should first choose to be in a market where high profitability is obtainable, and then choose their position (differentiation or cost leadership) within these markets.[4]

Figure 4.2 shows the cash flows over time for acquaintances, friends, and partners in conditions of low versus high demand heterogeneity. The vertical axes represent cash flow in dollars, while the horizontal axes again represent the market period. In the low heterogeneity condition, we observe that most of the cash flow comes from acquaintances. When heterogeneity is high, friends and partners come to dominate CPLV cash flows over time.

We cannot underestimate the importance of the sizable difference in cash flow between these two conditions. Considering that there is significant customer heterogeneity in most of the markets in our economies, the contrast illustrates both the considerable returns to relationship conversion and that those returns are downstream. Companies and shareholders who focus myopically on short-term cash flows and ROI will end up underinvesting in relationship development and leave considerable amounts of money on the table. We see this observation as consistent with business strategist Roger Martin's advocacy for the "age of customer capitalism."[5] Martin argues that a continual focus on shareholder value is impossible as stock prices are driven by expectations regarding the future that cannot be raised indefinitely, nor has a focus on shareholder value led to greater returns. Rather, Martin advocates for following the examples of companies like Procter & Gamble (we would add Amazon today) that make customer value and satisfaction top priorities, as these companies generate returns equal to or better than shareholder-focused companies.

Prescriptive Strategies

With these differences in cash flow in mind, we can use the CPLV model to look more closely at prescriptive strategies that increase the value of a customer portfolio. We start with the distinction between acquiring and retaining customers, which is at the heart of the distinction between offensive and defensive marketing strategies. Both strategies are essential to

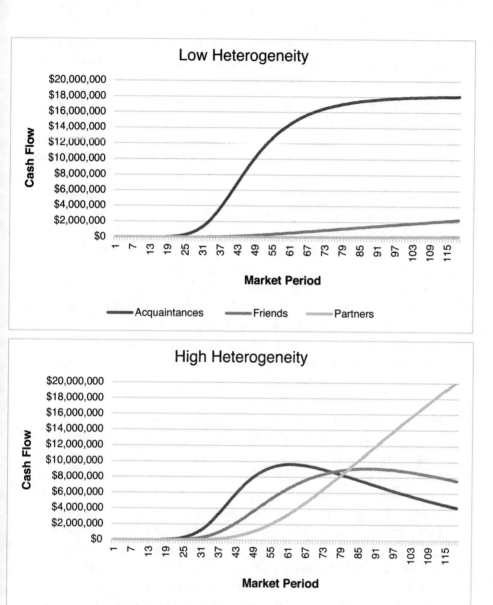

Figure 4.2

Cash flows over time in low versus high customer heterogeneity conditions.

effective portfolio management. In their simplest forms, offensive marketing focuses on increasing market size or market share, while defensive marketing focuses on reducing brand switching, or churn, either by delivering high satisfaction (giving customers a reason to stay) or by the creation of switching barriers (which make it more difficult for customers to leave).[6] Recognize, however, that both strategies lead to higher market share, albeit in different ways. Offense builds market share through the acquisition of new customers, typically during the growth phase of a product or service life cycle. Defense builds share later in a life cycle, typically through superior brand value propositions (customer satisfaction) and resulting retention.

But if competitors simply copy each other and follow the same strategies—that is, they invest equally in their capabilities—they should end up with equivalent financial results.[7] But what happens if one firm or brand can develop a sustainable advantage related to offense, defense, or relationship conversion? That is, the brand develops unique capabilities or a system of interconnected activities that become difficult or impossible to imitate.[8] And how much more profitable are these competitive advantages under conditions of low versus high heterogeneity? In the next section we explore how these strategies impact CPLV.

Simulating Acquisition, Defense, and Conversion Strategies

New customers in the CPLV model are either first-time customers who are just entering the market or customers acquired from a competitor. If both competitors invest equally in acquisition with equal effectiveness, they should gain roughly the same number of new customers in a market period, other things being equal. But if one of the competitors invests more or better than the other, it should acquire more customers. Customer acquisition strategies to attract new-to-the-market customers are about creating awareness, engagement, and trial through investments in advertising and distribution. Acquisition strategies to attract or "steal" customers from competitors involve developing more attractive brands through product and service development and advertising, often in combination with various forms of discount promotions.

If competitors invest equally in customer defense, this should also result in an equal number of customers retained versus lost in each period. By investing more in customer defense than competitors, a company stands to reduce switching probabilities versus competitors. The brand will retain more customers than competing brands and its market share increases. Companies may, for example, invest in discount promotions directed towards existing customers with high switching probabilities, although that means competing on price rather than quality. Another frequently used strategy is investment in the benefits of loyalty programs. As, however, customers are more likely to leave relationships due to dissatisfaction with product or service quality, ongoing quality improvement to reduce "things gone wrong" and increase "things gone right" is essential to customer satisfaction and retention. We return to this topic in more detail in chapter 6 when we describe satisfaction modeling.

In addition to acquisition and defense, companies may focus on creating an advantage in relationship conversion, which would include activities related specifically to increasing the probability of converting acquaintances to friends and friends to partners. Acquaintances may be educated regarding the higher quality or functionality of product and service offerings to appreciate the differentiation. Friends may be shown how a more customized offering is worth the investment in a partnership as customers adapt to a brand's ecosystem of products and services. Starbucks, for example, encourages its customers to use preorder and prepayment services in its mobile app, in addition to participation in its loyalty program. Relationship conversion is a natural development as markets mature and customers come to appreciate different product and service qualities and functionalities. In conditions of low customer heterogeneity, this conversion is slower and far less likely. As the low heterogeneity condition in figure 4.1 illustrates, the portfolio is dominated by acquaintances, relatively few of whom convert to friends and partners. When customer heterogeneity is high, conversion is faster and more likely, resulting in more friends and partners over time. A conversion strategy marginally increases these conversion rates.

To capture these three strategies, we formulated a response function for investments in acquisition, defense, and conversion activities as an S-shaped relationship, meaning that investments have a marginally increasing impact, followed by diminishing effects on customer acquisition, defense, and conversion, respectively. As these market activities require more specialized organizational capabilities, they should become more effective with increased investment before reaching the diminishing returns of their effectiveness. We simulated these strategies under low and high customer heterogeneity to illustrate their impact on CPLV. We defined *high investment*

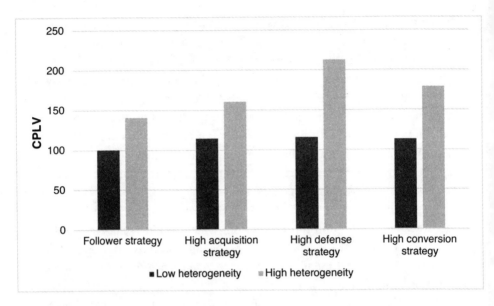

Figure 4.3
The impact of customer acquisition, defense, and conversion investments on CPLV.

strategies as a 10 percent increase in acquisition, defense, or conversion activities vis-à-vis the competition.

Figure 4.3 compares a *follower strategy* (equal investments in offense, defense, and conversion versus competitors) to the high investment strategies under low and high demand heterogeneity. As in previous scenarios, we keep economies of scale constant (50 percent reduction in unit cost over time, depending on volume). The vertical axis here represents the total CPLV across conditions. For comparison purposes, we index the dollar value of CPLV here at 100 for the follower strategy where heterogeneity is low as a baseline condition. The impacts for other conditions are then interpretable as percentage increases from this baseline. CPLV is naturally higher in the high heterogeneity follower condition, given the opportunities this presents to create friends and partners.

Notice how much CPLV grows for all three higher investment strategies versus the baseline when customer heterogeneity is high. This is especially the case for a defense focused strategy, where the increase in CPLV under low heterogeneity is 16 percent compared to an increase of over 100 percent for the high heterogeneity condition. The impact of defense on

CPLV is also marginally higher than the other strategies across the low heterogeneity conditions. Defensive strategies, especially in the presence of customer heterogeneity, have a tremendous payoff which is related to the value of retaining a larger volume of higher margin friends and partners in a portfolio. Granted, the outputs of these scenarios depend on the inputs used. But the observed relative importance of defense on CPLV is highly consistent with observed positive impacts of customer satisfaction on business performance. Strong brands deliver this customer satisfaction through ongoing efforts to continuously improve and innovate products and service processes thus increasing their relative attractiveness.

Both acquisition and conversion strategies also have a sizable impact on CPLV when customer heterogeneity is high. For acquisition, this reflects the fact that there is a larger population of acquaintances in a portfolio, which lowers unit costs and leads to larger populations of friends and partners. For the conversion strategy, the higher CPLV reflects the fact that a larger percentage of weaker customer relationships grow into stronger relationships with price premiums and higher margins. By extension, a combination of these strategies where a brand creates a competitive advantage with respect to customer acquisition, relationship defense, and relationship conversion adds tremendously to the lifetime value of a customer portfolio.

The Value of Relationship Leverage: Brand Extensions

Another strategy for increasing the value of a customer portfolio is to leverage stronger customer relationships by introducing *brand extensions*, as through the addition of new product and service offerings to a brand's ecosystem.[9] We extended the CPLV model to illustrate the value of brand extensions.

We specified the brand extension strategy as follows:

- We introduced a brand extension, or second product life cycle, to customers in period 70 of the brand's initial product life cycle. The price and cost of the new product were set at the same level as the first product.

- We assumed the same level of customer demand heterogeneity for both product categories.

- The costs of cross-selling the second product were set to $50, $10, and $5 for acquaintances, friends, and partners respectively as we expect marketing costs to decrease the more customers have adapted to a differentiated or customized brand offering.

- When customers are buying both products, retention increases 0.5 percent for friends and partners in the low heterogeneity market and 1.0 percent for friends and partners in the high heterogeneity market.
- The probability of adopting the second product in one period, once introduced, is 0.5 percent, 1.0 percent, and 1.5 percent for acquaintances, friends, and partners in the low heterogeneity market, and 0.5 percent, 2.0 percent, and 3.0 percent for acquaintances, friends, and partners in the high heterogeneity market.

We find that introducing a second product category increases the accumulated CPLV by only 4 percent when demand heterogeneity is low and the customer portfolio is dominated by acquaintances. When heterogeneity is high and the portfolio includes primarily strong (friend and partner) relationships, accumulated CPLV increases by 25 percent. The simple conclusion here is that, in the context of cross-selling product or service offerings, the lower marketing costs associated with a portfolio of closer customer relationships adds significantly to CPLV. The impact is much lower when cross-selling to acquaintances. When, for example, we add conditions where a firm gains a competitive advantage related to offense, defense, or conversion *and* it introduces a second product category, the biggest increase in CPLV occurs when a brand pursues a customer retention strategy (63 percent increase). The implication is that brand extension strategies are particularly profitable when customer demand is heterogeneous and firms invest in retention.

Market Shocks

One thing we have learned about our economies is that markets are inherently turbulent and subject to periodic and unexpected shocks. The CPLV model offers interesting insights when there are shocks to an economic system. Shocks occur when, for example, there are significant economic downturns and associated supply chain disruptions that categorically increase costs, require investments in technology or physical plants, or decrease what customers are willing to spend. Previous simulations of the model reveal how sudden cost increases drive large swings in the relative contribution of acquaintances, friends, and partners in a portfolio.[10] Although the cash flow from acquaintances may remain high, their contribution margins become a significant risk. Because the margins for acquaintances are relatively thin, sudden cost increases have more dramatic effects on their contributions compared to friends' and partners'. This creates scenarios where friends become the most valuable relationship in a portfolio, as they effectively balance risk (higher margins than acquaintances) and return (greater scale than partners).

We extend the model here to a question:

How do investments in CPM strategies aimed at creating a competitive advantage with respect to offense (acquisition), defense (retention), and relationship conversion protect and preserve cash flows in the face of market turbulence? In this case, we constructed a market where the price that customers pay drops precipitously or shocks the market. We simulated the market shock as follows:

- In period 70, all prices dropped by 20 percent, after which prices gradually return to their previous levels.
- All other parameters were the same as in the one-product market defined above.

Figure 4.4 shows the total CPLV (in dollars) for the follower strategy and when Brand A invests disproportionately in customer acquisition, relationship defense, and relationship conversion, all with the addition of the price cut. The vertical axis again represents total CPLV, benchmarked here at 100 for the low heterogeneity follower strategy where all competitors have the same capabilities. The first observation is, once again, the main effect of customer heterogeneity on CPLV. Even in the face of a significant price shock, CPLV is much higher when opportunities exist to create closer, more profitable relationships with customers where margins are more protected. The interesting result here, however, is how the defensive and offensive strategies add value while the conversion strategy results in no material improvement to CPLV.

This finding is the result of an interesting dynamic. Both the offensive and defensive strategies, as noted earlier, increase the size of a portfolio, albeit in different ways. Offense does so by acquiring newer customers—that is, adding water to the leaky bucket. Defense does so by limiting defections or plugging holes in the bucket. The conversion strategy operates differently, where the focus is on increasing the marginal conversion rate rather than increasing the size of the portfolio through acquisition or retention. Market share growth is negligible in this case, meaning that both the

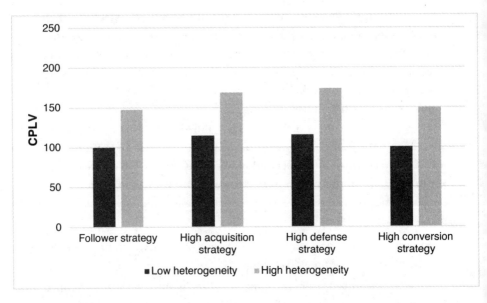

Figure 4.4
The impact of acquisition, defense, and conversion on CPLV with a market shock (20 percent price cut).

follower and conversion strategies have higher unit costs structures compared to the offensive and defensive strategies. The conversion strategy fails to achieve the cost advantage that the other strategies enjoy. When the price cut is added to the increased costs of conversion, it offsets the primary advantage of the conversion strategy, which is a marginal increase in friends and partners relative to acquaintances.

Put differently, a strategy that focuses myopically on a "conversion advantage" without gaining a cost advantage through portfolio growth is relatively ineffective in the face of a significant price reduction. This explains why the defensive strategy is also the dominant strategy in figure 4.3, where the price shock is absent and customer heterogeneity is high. While an offensive strategy is focused more on scale, and a conversion strategy is focused more on margins, a retention strategy leverages both.

Chapter Summary

Our insights into CPM over the past 20 years have benefited greatly from our modeling of CPLV, or customer portfolio lifetime value. By simulating differences in relationship conversion, churn, competitive capabilities, and other moving parts of a market, the model illustrates how a wide range of market conditions impact both the overall value of a portfolio and the relative importance of different business strategies. It underscores the importance of both cost advantage and differentiation toward increasing CPLV and the value of a large leaky bucket of customers, where some customers are constantly churning while others become more profitable, closer relationships.

A primary takeaway from the results presented here is how the heterogeneity of markets and resulting opportunities for brands to differentiate or customize offerings to create more friends and partners impacts the value of a portfolio. In commodity markets where customer portfolios are dominated by weaker, acquaintance relationships, a volume-based strategy that relies on creating economies of scale is more attractive. But as market heterogeneity increases, friendships and partnerships grow and become the dominant contributors to the value of a portfolio. When a firm creates competitive advantages with respect to offense or customer acquisition, relationship defense, relationship conversion, or multiple of these, it creates important dynamics. While offensive and defensive strategies benefit the most from growing the size of a portfolio and reducing unit costs, the defensive and conversion strategies benefit the most from creating stronger relationships and higher profit per customer. As a result, a defense-focused strategy has the greatest overall impact on CPLV. Introducing a second product or cross-selling opportunity midway through the product life cycle increases CPLV by leveraging the lower marketing costs associated with stronger customer relationships. And when we shock the market by introducing a significant price cut in the middle of the product life cycle, the unit cost advantages of the offensive and defensive strategies serve to buffer the value of a portfolio from market turbulence.

Within the framework of CPM, the implementation of these strategies requires an underlying commitment to using customer data to obtain insight into how to take advantage of the heterogeneity of customer needs and successfully differentiate and customize product and service offerings. In the next two chapters we turn to the data and predictive modeling that is instrumental to that process.

5   CPM Analytics

Basic Workflows

CPM analytics is a class of data and methodological systems or work-flows, some more generally related to market research and some specific to CPM, designed to transform customer data into effective organizational decisions, processes, and resulting portfolio growth. The more customers acquired, the more candidates for friendships and partnerships, the higher cash flow these customers produce, and the longer they are retained, all of which adds to the value of a portfolio. As CPM is an organization-wide approach to marketing, the impact of CPM analytics spreads beyond tra-ditional marketing to top management and other business functions. This view of marketing is consistent with what previous authors have referred to as taking a *market orientation*—that is, a view of marketing that embraces both a customer and competitor focus.[1] It also means that the specifics of CPM analytics will vary considerably from firm to firm based on the size of the firm, its customer base, and how resources and activities are organized across functions. It follows that the specifics of CPM analytics will change over time as firms adapt their strategies and ways of organizing.

Figure 5.1 divides the structure of CPM analytics into three basic work-flows. First is the development of a customer database and generation of descriptive statistics regarding relationship segments and the factors, or variables, that directly or indirectly impact those segments. The second workflow is developing an understanding of the basic causal mechanisms that relate firm and market activities to customer perceptions and behav-ior and subsequently to business performance and portfolio growth. We focus on how a brand's product and service attributes and benefits impact the customer experience in the form of customer satisfaction, and how

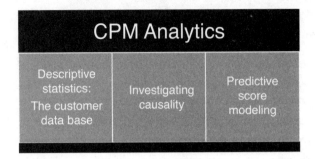

Figure 5.1
Basic structure of CPM analytics.

customers satisfaction in turn impacts business performance. The third workflow involves the use of customer data to develop predictive score models regarding customers' expected behavior and their responses to market-related activities.

The main point of departure of CPM analytics from other CRM systems is its grounding in relationship segmentation. The descriptive statistics, causality, and predictive scoring are all grounded in how one defines strangers (prospective customers), acquaintances, friends, and partners. What drives customer satisfaction for friends may be very different from what drives satisfaction for acquaintances or partners as the value propositions are different. This means that the corresponding implications for each relationship segment may be categorized by their impact on customer acquisition, defense, leverage, and conversion.

Descriptive Statistics: The Customer Database

The relevant customer data for CPM analytics is usually found in multiple data sources that need to be integrated, engineered, and maintained. An important task in data engineering is developing systems and procedures for continuous data streams and data quality control. Which data sources to integrate depends on what data is available and what data is needed. Unfortunately, there is no universal prescription for how a customer database should be constructed. We do, however, believe in a set of guiding principles related to constructing smart variables, integrating data from multiple sources, embracing variability, and maintaining data quality.

Principle #1: Construct Smart Variables

So, what do we mean by *smart variables*? Market researchers often describe their task as transforming raw data into meaningful information and using that information to make decisions and improve processes. Data and information may inform decisions, but managers and executives make decisions. The construction of smart variables is a process of translating raw data (e.g., transactional customer records, volume purchased, price paid, frequency of visits, complaints) into more meaningful variables (e.g., relationship segments, loyal customers, switchers). A key capability is the identification and operationalization of the variables needed to succeed in the CPM analytic workflows and their output. This requires a deep understanding of how data is generated, how analytics work, and how customers behave and respond to market activities. Firms should put considerable thought into how raw data is transformed into meaningful variables.

Perhaps the most important example of converting descriptive data into smart variables within the framework of CPM is the allocation of customers into the relationship segments described previously. The variables used to classify customers into these segments depend on what data is, or can be made, available. For our building materials retailer from chapter 2, we combined transactional data (share of wallet) and survey data regarding brand preference to create meaningful relationship segments (low volume acquaintances, high volume acquaintances, friends, and partners). But this is just one example. Transactional data may be used to create other variables, such as the breadth of product or service categories purchased. Grocery customers may be categorized by how many and which categories they shop for (e.g., fresh fruit and vegetables, fresh meat and fish, bakery, dairy products, hygiene products, etc.) while bank customers may be categorized by services used (e.g., checking account, brokerage account, loan account, etc.). Such categorizations help us understand how many different connections customers have with a company or brand, the types of connections they use, methods of communicating (phone, emails, chats), app use, loyalty program use, and so forth.

For a grocery retailer, acquaintances might be defined as customers who purchase from at least one product category in the last month. Friends may be defined as customers who have purchased from multiple product categories in the last month and are connected in more than one way to the retailer, as through a loyalty program or downloaded app. Meanwhile, partners may be defined by having made purchases in even more product categories with even more connections, such as their participation in feedback systems such as online reviews. With these definitions in place, the retailer can monitor the conversion of some customers from acquaintances to friends and friends to partners. What is important is that the criteria used makes sense to the retailer or company based on its understanding of its customers and its business. For our building materials retailer, the definitions emerged from our discussions with management—what made sense and what they could work with.

How, for example, might one construct a variable to capture whether a specific customer is new, an ongoing or active part of a portfolio, or estranged? The first step is to define what you mean by customer, be it an individual, a household, or the buying center in a larger organization. This defines the unit of analysis, or the row in the customer database (spreadsheet), and the individual or individuals that have defined roles in the customer relationship (e.g., accounting, sales, service). Defining individuals and roles is important as it captures how the customer interacts with the company or brand. The second step is to define when a relationship with a customer starts and when it ends. For acquaintances or transactional customers, the start of a relationship would be the first transaction. But for how long after this transaction should the customer be defined as active as opposed to inactive? The fact that customers vary in their purchase patterns complicates the issue, since some customers transact weekly while others may transact monthly or even annually.

We have found that many companies use customers' historical purchase patterns to define "active." If, for example, a weekly customer has been inactive for months, the customer is no longer active, while a monthly customer is considered active for a longer period. Thus, the descriptive statistic labeling a lost customer may vary by customer history. If and when they return, they will be counted as a new customer, be they truly new or a returning customer. This is important information when we describe changes in the customer portfolio and evaluate the use of market activities to grow the portfolio. For example, in evaluating a win-back program where the purpose is to reactivate previous customers, lapsed weekly customers would receive the program or promotion before lapsed monthly customers.

Predictors are another important subset of smart variables in a database. Predictors signal, for example, when repurchase behavior or churn are imminent. For online retailers like Amazon, placing several options in a digital shopping cart before deciding signals an imminent purchase, while a decline in purchase frequency or a negative review of a recently purchased product may signal an imminent departure. Using multiple variables within a predictive model may also be used to generate more summary predictive variables, such as retention probabilities. Developing good predictors is one of the key workflows in CPM analytics, a topic we elaborate on later in the chapter.

Another class of smart, descriptive variables includes constructs such as relationship strength, customer satisfaction, customer loyalty, and brand preference. These more abstract variables are best measured indirectly through a set of measurable indicators or variables. In the American Customer Satisfaction Index methodology, for example, the "perceived quality" of a product or service brand is calculated using an index of three survey measures: (1) an overall evaluation of quality, (2) an evaluation of customization or how well the brand fits the customer's personal requirements, and (3) an evaluation of reliability, or how often things go wrong. Overall customer satisfaction is measured as an index of three other survey measures: (1) overall satisfaction, (2) whether the experience falls short of or exceeds expectations, and (3) brand performance versus an ideal product or service in the category.[2]

The value of using indices of multiple survey items is that they provide more sensitive and reliable measures of the constructs. The academic literature is replete with usable definitions of key constructs and the survey items used to measure them. The use of multiple item indices to measure constructs like quality and satisfaction becomes centrally important in the models and measurement systems used to predict business performance. For a given relationship segment, how do perceptions of product quality, service quality, and price impact satisfaction, retention, and subsequent business performance? And how do perceptions of product quality, service quality, and price relate to improvements in more specific attributes and benefits?

The critical success factor, as mentioned, is not just how to turn data into meaningful information but how to turn that information into meaningful decisions and better processes. The CPM analytics team must develop a deep understanding of what data is most valuable to the top management team, the marketing function, and other critical business functions. The users of the analytics need not be experts at producing the analytics. They do, however, need to understand what the output means. What, for example, do we mean by "impact," such as the impact of satisfaction on actual retention? The reader may recall (from that statistics class they would like to forget) how a regression model works, where satisfaction may be an independent or explanatory variable used to explain loyalty or retention as a dependent variable. The beta coefficients in regression modeling indicate the average increase (i.e., impact) in a dependent variable (e.g., retention) based on a given increase in an independent variable (e.g., satisfaction).

Our observation is that many companies hire data analysts in the hope of developing meaningful metrics through machine learning and other sophisticated methods. But those efforts will be less than successful unless the analysts truly understand both customer behavior and what management is trying to accomplish with the data.

Principle #2: Integrate Data Sources

The real value of a customer database comes from assembling and integrating data from multiple sources. Describing, explaining, and predicting human behavior, in this case customer behavior, is one of the most complex endeavors in management and the social sciences. Ideally the *data sources* would include information on past behavior; perceptions of constructs like quality, satisfaction, and relationship strength; and the external competitive and market factors that influence customer behaviors, thinking, and feeling. We break these data sources down into five basic categories: transactional data, interaction data, customer survey data, location data, and competitor data.

Transactional Data   Transactional data is a record of customers' past purchasing behavior, including records related to payments, products and services purchased, time of purchase, and location (i.e., invoice, receipts, tabs). These records are typically collected for accounting purposes rather than predicting and explaining customer behavior. But CPM analytics uses this transaction data to inform us about customers. Whereas transactional data for accounting purposes should be as error-free as possible, transactional data for CPM purposes need not be as accurate, and probably will never be.

Which variables to develop depends on how the data is to be used. When predicting future cash flow (i.e., customer lifetime value, or CLV), we want variables to inform the expected size and timing of future purchases. If a customer has reliably purchased $10 of a product or service every Saturday for the last 100 weeks, the prediction is that they will do the same next week. If, however, the customer has spent between $1 and $50 every Saturday, the predicted level of spending will be an average around a range or interval that is estimated using simple statistics. Likewise, if the customer spends the same amount but on an irregular basis, the transactional data will predict an average time between purchases and the range or interval around that estimate. The statistics inform us about the uncertainty we can expect to gain from the transactional data.

This uncertainty may be reduced by gathering more data from other sources. This may include recording and understanding which product or service categories customers purchase. One retailer found that its customers could be grouped into four clusters based on the similarity of the types of products they purchased.[3] One cluster purchased primarily family items, including plastic folders, drawing materials, candy, and toys. Another cluster used the retailer to purchase party-related products, while a third and fourth cluster purchased decorations and household products, respectively. Individual customers could then be described based on the one or two categories they typically purchased within each cluster. This information was used to differentiate email promotions to stimulate purchases in categories customers were already buying and stimulate purchases in related categories customer were not buying.

Interaction Data   Interaction data is information regarding the contact or touchpoints that customers have with a company or brand. The volume of these interactions is accelerating with the diffusion of digital platforms and omnichannel marketing. Interaction data records encounters initiated either by the brand or by the customer, keeping track of the time, channel or touchpoint, and type of interaction. The recent popularity of *customer journey mapping* is a case in point. Journey maps track the touchpoints with customers, "moments of truth" in the process, and interactions in need of improvement. We elaborate on journey mapping when discussing customer satisfaction modeling in chapter 6.

Numerous sources of interaction data are typically available in a company's CRM system and are a valuable way to better understand customer needs. Exploring transactional data related to customers' chosen locations or channels, loyalty program usage, service requests, inbound communication (customer to company, such as requests, complaints, web traffic), outbound communication (company to customer, such as emails, texts, mail), and physical contacts (such as store visits or sales calls) is a good place to start. Before jumping into all the data, however, one should think carefully through what the organization needs and will actually use.

Consider a fitness center that uses transaction data to predict customer defections or churn. A predictive model estimates each customer's exit probability based on their pattern of visits, length of membership, and descriptive variables that include age, gender, and location. The model accurately predicts when customers are likely to churn and provides insight into the underlying causes. A close examination of exit and usage patterns revealed a large difference between those who regularly use the membership and those who do not. Qualitative interviews with members from both groups added more insight. The first group had an established, healthy lifestyle with regular exercise, which they simply continued upon becoming members. The second group started their membership hoping it would lead to a healthier lifestyle. Once the fitness center understood this, personal trainers proactively followed up with programming for members in the second group. The predictive model both identifies members of each segment and triggers programming for customers in the want-to-be healthier segment.

Customer Survey Data   Transactional and interaction data benefit from the addition of survey data to better understand customer behavior. Through surveys we better understand customer perceptions, thoughts, and feelings. In essence, the addition of survey data combines psychological data with behavioral data obtained from transactional and interaction data. Survey data and methodologies have a long tradition in the social sciences and marketing research, dating back to the pioneering work of George Gallup who founded the American Institute of Public Opinion, the predecessor to today's Gallup, Inc., in 1935. Gallup developed a successful statistical method of survey sampling for measuring public opinion. The method was widely used not only for measuring public opinion but also to produce a representative description of attitudes, needs, preferences, and other psychological variables and, of course, for marketing. The American Customer Satisfaction Index relies on the same basic principle of surveying representative samples of US consumers.[4]

While survey sampling methods provide representative descriptions of a population, they do not measure changes at the individual customer level over time. In a traditional survey sample, we may find that a group of satisfied customers report visiting a retailer more frequently than a group of dissatisfied customers. One might infer that an increase in satisfaction will lead to an increase in visit frequency, presuming that the dissatisfied customers simply had a poor service experience. The real reason may be that the two groups have very different needs. The higher satisfaction group may value something the retailer does well, such as assortment, while the lower satisfaction group may value something at which the retailer does not excel, such as convenience. Sampling methodologies will not tell us that. Rather, by tracking the same customer over time we can directly estimate the effect of changes in customer satisfaction on visit frequency. Whereas statistical sampling provides cross-sectional data points, the continuous measuring of customers provides a time series of psychological and behavioral data at the individual level. This gives us a much richer set of data to understand all the variation that exists in the customer data.

Location Data   Location data, more specifically the customer's location including where they live and work, is a particular type of transactional data that is useful toward understanding the external or environmental factors that affect customers. Location data can be obtained through public records and many countries provide information regarding what type of dwelling the customer lives in and its market value. Adding demographic information regarding neighborhoods, roads, public transportation, recreational areas, and other publicly available information helps to build customer profiles.

For brick-and-mortar retailers and other chains, an important application of this data is the estimation of how far customers are willing to travel to visit a physical facility, which can be used to evaluate the attractiveness of new locations or how moving a location will affect customers. A private medical center used these statistics to identify superior locations it would have otherwise missed. In one case, it had the option of establishing a new location on either the north side or the south side of a river in a central business district. Estimations based on available statistics showed that the location on the south side would attract 20 percent more customers than the north side location simply because it was both within an acceptable travel distance for most people and closer than its main competitor.

Mobility data—that is, data regarding the time, effort, and risks (accidents) related to different modes of travel—is an increasing source of relevant data for many companies. This data is being used to better understand what types of both current and future mobility—from driving one's own vehicle to biking or walking to riding in an autonomous robo-shuttle or robo-pod—are better fits for customers in different types of cities.[5] When evaluating a new distribution outlet, mobility data estimates both distance to current customers and the potential to attract new customers based on traffic density.

Competitor Data Customers implicitly or explicitly choose between brands they have bought before and competing brands. The relative attractiveness of a brand is clarified through detailed information regarding customers' competitive sets. Competitor data is available through many different sources from annual reports, websites, media reports, and direct observation (visiting competitors' stores or websites). Annual reports for public companies often provide excellent descriptions of competitors' strengths, weaknesses, and strategies for their own shareholders. Joining a competitor's loyalty program or customer clubs is another form of competitive benchmarking. The diffusion of machine learning and AI will no doubt make the collection of competitor data that much easier, where machines are trained to create variables to describe competitors' product and service categories, prices, locations, brand image, advertising, sales, stock prices, etc. Of course, competitors will be using the same type of technology to understand and profile your company and brands. Competitor data can be connected to information about individual customers in the customer database. For each customer in the database, we can identify the competitors that are closest to their address or in their "evoked set" of considered brands to make predictions based on the attractiveness of competitors and therefore differentiate marketing activities.

Principle #3: Embrace Variability

Think about the person who tried to wade across a stream with an "average" depth of two feet but still drowned. The point is that averages can be very misleading. Nevertheless, averages are what is typical in reports on customer satisfaction, brand attitudes, churn, advertising awareness, and other variables related to marketing and customer portfolio management.

Say, for example, that a customer satisfaction survey reports a change in average customer satisfaction from 7.0 to 7.1 on a 10-point scale. Including variability, the report adds that the proportion of customers responding below 5 has increased from 10 percent to 15 percent, and the proportion of customers responding 8 and above has increased from 15 percent to 20 percent. Adding information on the variability in satisfaction scores provides more diagnostic value and would point to the need to better understand the differences between the low and the high satisfaction customers.

Variability is also needed to infer causality between a market intervention and changes in customer perceptions and behavior. If a company spends the exact same amount of advertising with the same message in every period (i.e., day, week, or month), one cannot infer the causal effect of different levels of advertising spending or advertising messages on behavior or perceptions. Sales may go up or down while the advertising remains constant, but we can't infer if advertising has an effect or not. As most companies vary their advertising spend and messaging across periods, we can use this natural variation to infer if an increase in sales (or other variables) is correlated with changes in advertising.

We can also induce variability in our data through various forms of experimentation. With experiments, we can, for example, increase or decrease advertising in one group (e.g., geographic area, segment, etc.) and compare areas with respect to differences in sales or other variables. A retailer that practiced an always-on weekly promotion (i.e., no variation in advertising) conducted a field experiment where advertising was turned off and on in selected regions. It found that there was no difference in sales between the experiment group (where advertising was turned off and on) and the control group (the rest of the regions).[6] Thus, advertising had no effect on sales and the retailer could reduce or remove this expense without losing sales.

A/B testing, as when testing two versions of a website or email communication, has become a very popular and relevant method for inducing variability. Different versions of an email (e.g., versions A and B) are sent to sample customers and the emails with most openings or clicks are deployed to the whole population of targeted customers. The important point is to embrace variability and include as many sources of that variability as possible to better understand how a portfolio of brands and competitors' offerings impacts a portfolio of customers. Thus, when we construct customer databases for analytical purposes, we embrace data with variability.

While measures of central tendency (such as means and medians) communicate average or typical values, measures of dispersion (such as ranges and standard deviations) communicate the variability in descriptive variables. It is this variability that allows us to group customers into different categories based on descriptive statistics. Sales revenues from different relationship segments may be used to group customers into different demographic subsegments, such as sales revenues for acquaintances across age groups. Likewise, customer acquisition rates may be used to subsegment customers based on interaction channels. This information informs managers and guides the development of a customer portfolio in CPM. It helps managers to direct marketing and other business activities more effectively, since customers with a higher propensity to churn (acquaintances) activate one set of retention activities, while customers with a lower propensity to churn (friends and partners) activate a very different retention strategy.

Principle #4: Data Quality and Control

When constructing a database to manage a customer portfolio, there is no tradeoff for data quality and control. The database needs to be maintained and use a consistent format. One might assume that databases are relatively unaffected by human error, but unfortunately that is not the case. Humans make changes to how data is computed, stored, and ultimately used. And they do so without necessarily informing others what changes have been made. An important principle in CPM analytics is to be a control freak with respect to data quality.

One example of data failure is when companies change numerical product codes. An existing product could be mistaken for a new product unless we inform the system to treat the old code and the new code as the same product. Another example is when media agencies change how they report media spending from weekly to biweekly reports, where statistical modeling may erroneously assume that the spending is every second week and not every week, leading to inaccurate estimates. Yet another example is when someone forgets to input their market activities, such as customer interventions, into a database. If a sales representative forgets to register a "positive customer visit" or "price cut" that leads to a transaction, the underlying model will underestimate the effect of the intervention.

Data quality management refers to the process of ensuring the accuracy, completeness, consistency, and reliability of data. This includes data profiling which involves analyzing data to gain insights into its quality characteristics, such as completeness, consistency, uniqueness, and validity. What data anomalies, inaccuracies, or inconsistencies need to be corrected or removed from the database? Data management includes the establishment of defined rules, standards, roles, and responsibilities, and enforcing data standards and best practices.

We have found that adherence to these four principles—constructing smart variables, integrating data sources, embracing variability, and being a control freak on data quality—are essential to the construction of a strong customer database. They enhance our ability to connect descriptive statistics to *key business performance indicators* (KPIs) including sales revenue, customer acquisition rates, customer defection rates, brand strength, and the return on market activities. Comparing current performance with historical data or industry benchmarks allows businesses to identify areas of strength and areas in need of improvement.

Investigating Causality

With high quality customer data in hand, we can describe the behavior of different relationship segments. The problem is that we do not necessarily know what factors are driving that behavior. To invest in the right market interventions, we need to know the causal relationship involving interventions and their effect on customers. Understanding the "why" requires an understanding of *causality*. The philosopher John Stuart Mill stated that a causal relationship exists when: (1) the cause precedes the effect, (2) the cause is related to the effect, and (3) we can find no plausible alternative explanation for the effect other than the cause.[7] The gold standard for testing causality is an experiment where a treatment is provided in a controlled setting, where no other variables are involved, and the result of the treatment is measured against a control group that does not receive the treatment. The difference between the result for the treatment group and the result for the control group is the effect of the treatment. And because participation in the two groups is randomized, we can rule out alternative explanations.

Proving causality using naturally occurring data is far more difficult if not impossible as there will always be variables unaccounted for. It is possible, however, to support causality using such data. Consider the natural variation in customer experiences and resulting perceptions of product and service quality, customer satisfaction, and retention. Satisfaction models hypothesize that perceptions of quality impact satisfaction, while satisfaction in turn impacts retention (quality → satisfaction → retention).[8] That is, quality perceptions cause retention not directly, but, rather, indirectly through customers' overall evaluations of their satisfaction with a brand. Statistically, this means the impact of quality perceptions on retention is mediated by customer satisfaction.

A straightforward statistical test of mediation in this case involves the series of regression models illustrated in figure 5.2, where the independent

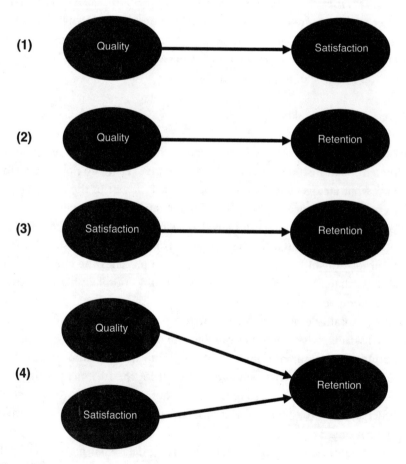

Figure 5.2
Testing for mediation.

variables in the regressions are on the left and the dependent variables are on the right. The models include testing for: (1) the impact of quality on satisfaction, (2) the impact of quality on retention, (3) the impact of satisfaction on retention, and (4) the impact of both quality and satisfaction on retention in the same model. The first step is to establish significant positive relationships involving all two-way relationships (models 1–3). If those tests are all positive, the second step is to use both quality and satisfaction as independent variables to explain retention in a multivariate regression (model 4). When both quality and satisfaction are used to predict retention, if the impact of satisfaction remains strong and positive while the impact of quality either becomes nonsignificant or significantly reduced, the results support a causal relation where quality impacts retention either completely or partly *through* customer satisfaction.[9] Full mediation supports a simple causal relationship where quality → satisfaction → retention.

The use of causal modeling methodologies in academic and applied research, and satisfaction modeling in particular, has allowed researchers to test much larger networks of relationships using perceptions of product and service quality, price or value, and switching costs to predict customer satisfaction and subsequent business performance metrics such as retention. Research on the evolution of loyalty intentions suggests that the impact of quality and price on loyalty is more direct early in a product or service life cycle when customers are still forming their overall evaluations and brand concepts. As the life cycle matures, customers develop well-formed evaluations of their consumption experiences. As a result, the impact of price and quality on loyalty is mediated by these evaluations.[10] The implication for CPM is that the causal models used in CPM analytics will vary with the strength of the relationship. As acquaintances dominate early in a new product or service life cycle, quality and cost will have more direct impacts on retention. As friends and partners grow over time, customer satisfaction will come to mediate the impact of quality and cost factors on retention.

Another common approach to supporting causality when using natural data is the use of control variables to eliminate alternative explanations for an observed relationship. Consider a positive correlation between digital channel (search engine) advertising and observed new customer sales. A positive correlation between X (search-advertising expenditures) and Y (new customer sales) does not presume a causal relationship, as other variables may explain the variation. The brand may simply advertise more in

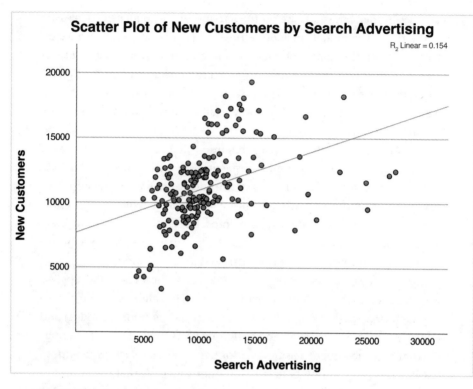

Figure 5.3
Investments in digital channel advertising versus new customer sales without control variables.

historically high-volume seasons where the *seasonality* (time of year), not the advertising, explains the sales. In figure 5.3, the scatter plot relating these two variables shows a regression line or average impact of weekly investments in Google advertising on the number of new customers for an e-commerce brand. The plot shows impact when only these two variables are considered. When a control variable is added to account for seasonality the regression line becomes flat and insignificant. Rather than concluding that an increase in advertising increases sales, the explanation is that the brand advertised more in some seasons and less in others where the ad spending paralleled purchasing patterns. The results undermine any conclusion that the Google advertising was driving sales.

Psychologist Kurt Lewin made famous the quote that "there is nothing more practical than a good theory."[11] Our causal inferences and the hypotheses regarding why customers behave the way they do benefit greatly from good theory. In causal analytics we are not only interested in estimating the size of the effect between X and Y but we also want to understand why X is causing Y. That is, what is the causal explanation for the effect? When we know why X is creating an effect, we can be more innovative in developing effective interventions. For example, if we know that the effect of advertising is mediated through higher top-of-mind awareness, as was the case for Scottish Widows, we can use advertising to create a more vivid image in customers' minds. If, alternatively, the effect is mediated by the importance of a particular product or service feature, as was the case for Nike running shoes, we would focus advertising on the unique brand characteristic to bolster brand preference. The relevant causality would initiate different advertising strategies in the two scenarios.

Predictive Score Modeling

With good customer data and a working knowledge of the causal inferences to explain customer behavior, CPM analytics rests on *predictive score modeling*, or *predictive scoring*, to manage ongoing market activities, from improvements in product or service quality to the effectiveness of email communication and sales calls. Although predicting a future event and explaining a causal relationship rely on the same data and statistical techniques, the modeling process is substantially different.[12] Predictive score models aim to provide the value of a yet to be observed variable Y based on observed variable X. In our context, for example, we want to predict if a customer is likely to churn based on a set of observations we have made (e.g., prior churn, transactions, customer satisfaction, switching costs, etc.). Or we may want to predict whether customers in a particular relationship segment are more or less likely to be interested in buying a related (bundled) product or service, or even if they are more or less likely to respond to a particular promotion.

In predictive scoring, we are not interested in understanding why—that is, the causal mechanisms that connect X to Y. When prediction is the only goal, we look for any independent variable that is associated with the dependent variable whether or not there is a good explanation for the connection. Our only criterion is that the independent variables must be known prior to knowing the dependent or predicted variable. In causal analytics, in contrast, we want to include variables and constructs that allow us to understand and infer why independent variables impact a dependent variable.

The diffusion of machine learning tools has in many ways revolutionized how companies can use big data to improve their businesses through better predictions of customer behavior and other important aspects of business performance. Machine learning simply means that computers abstract stored data into concepts and identify (learn) patterns that describe the data. It is also important to know that researchers in the statistical community have published thousands of algorithms in open communities and made them available to other researchers and practitioners. If someone, for example, has developed a good algorithm for identifying a satisfied customer based on written emails to a company, there is probably an algorithm available for this in the machine learning community. In this way, the time needed for developing good algorithms is dramatically reduced, and because researchers share their experiences, the algorithms will continue to improve.[13]

Recall the business school that developed a model for predicting students likely to transfer in the first year of their bachelor programs. With the help of the model the school identified potential transfers early in the first semester so that corrective interventions could target those students. A valuable data source was found in the learning system students logged into. This system generated several variables including the number of days logged in, clustering (lumpiness) of the login dates, frequency of logins, and how long (minutes) they stayed logged in. Background variables like age, grades from high school, gender, and the student's home state were collected from the student administration system. This model predicted 68 percent correctly at day 100 of the first semester as to whether the student would defect.

Organizational deployment of prediction models means that the model is implemented systematically, where new input data is generated continuously and the model is making ongoing predictions either in the form of a categorical variable (e.g., the customer is in a new relationship segment or has defected) or a numeric value (e.g., predicted sales). The predictions trigger different types of activities for the different segments. In the business school example, the predictions triggered a set of contact activities with students the model had identified as potential defectors. The bottom line is that both causal inferences and predictive modeling are critically important toward a firm's efforts to convert customers to stronger relationships, defend those relationships, and motivate customers to purchase more of a brand's product and service offerings.

Chapter Summary

When assembling the core analytics behind CPM we break the basic workflows down into three key functions: construction of the database for descriptive statistics, understanding the causal inferences that link different variables in the dataset, and running the predictive scoring models that inform management decisions and improve market-related processes. Much of what is described here will be familiar to those with well-developed CRM systems and data. The main takeaway, and what makes CPM analytics different, is that data construction, inferencing, and modeling all rest on a relationship segmentation scheme and the importance of understanding the lifetime value of relationship segments.

While the depth and breadth of customer databases vary widely from organization to organization, we have found that the same basic principles hold: (1) construct smart—that is, informative—variables, (2) integrate different data sources to create more valuable information, (3) embrace the variability in data in order to capture the variability in customer experiences, and (4) maintain data quality and control. Causal inferences, studied both in academic and applied research, help us to understand why changes in some variables affect changes in others. Predictive models provide values for future customer behavior (or other relevant customer variables) based on what is known today. CPM analytics thus allows us to describe, understand, and predict customer behavior across relationship segments. In chapter 6, we bring data and analytics together to provides explicit management recommendations related to customer acquisition, relationship defense, and relationship conversion.

6 Linking CPM Strategies to Business Performance

Given the value of customer acquisition, relationship defense, relationship conversion and relationship leverage within CPM, one would presume that firms routinely set goals related to these strategies and use customer insight to achieve them. Yet there remains a significant gap between the customer experience that executives believe they provide and what their companies actually provide.[1] Why is this the case? The reasons are complex and likely reflective of siloed organizational structures where customer-related goals become lost in translation. But we suspect there is another important reason: managers and executives believe they are achieving CPLV growth, albeit indirectly. They respond to customer needs and wants through ongoing product and service development, innovation, and continuous improvement efforts, expecting a larger and more profitable customer portfolio to follow. Yet this approach is no substitute for having explicit and measurable goals related to customer acquisition, defense, conversion, and leverage.

Closing the gap requires knowing how to measure and manage the customer experience and understanding where to allocate limited resources across a portfolio of weaker to stronger customer relationships. This requires linking continuous improvement and innovation to increases in customer satisfaction and loyalty for each of the relationship segments in your portfolio. Here in chapter 6, we review the basic principles of customer satisfaction measurement and management and provide an application to a segment of friends for a tire manufacturer. We use this case to illustrate the importance of interpreting the output of the analytics, where a focus on absolute performance may be very different from a focus on performance relative to a competitor. We end with a discussion of how to link this modeling to business performance to better understand the ROI of any investments in particular relationship segments. The process starts, however, with understanding how different types of satisfaction measures serve very different purposes.

Customer Satisfaction: Transactional or Cumulative?

In our interactions with managers and executives, we have found it important to emphasize how the construct of customer satisfaction is measured in two very different ways.[2] Early satisfaction research focused on a customer's evaluation of a particular product transaction, episode, or service encounter, called *transaction-specific satisfaction*. Airlines and hotel companies routinely ask customers to evaluate their most recent flight experience or hotel stay. More recent research has focused on *cross-transactional* or *cumulative customer satisfaction*, defined as a customer's overall evaluation of their experience to date with a product or service provider. While the measures are more complementary than competing, their distinction is often misunderstood in practice.

Transactional measures of satisfaction are particularly useful when designing and managing product or service encounters or service processes, as through *customer journey mapping*. They help companies like Amazon develop high-performance transaction systems that other companies emulate. Journey mapping is hardly a recent practice. Service companies including Disney and SAS have used journey maps for decades to identify steps in the customer service process in need of improvement, be it the Disney "orbit" or the "moments of truth" at SAS.[3] Journey mapping has taken on added popularity of late with the evolution of digital transactions and e-commerce. The advantage of journey maps is that they visualize the process customers go through and track their experience at different touchpoints or micro-moments in the process. In our teaching of journey mapping, we have found that developing a map typically involves the following general steps: (1) market segmentation, by relationship strength, needs, or both (2) identification and definition of the touchpoints (e.g., for an online retailer, that may be seeing an ad, assessing a website, researching reviews, filling and editing a virtual basket, checkout, shipping, tracking, and delivery), (3) setting goals for the touchpoints, (4) using customer research, surveys, or online reviews to assess satisfaction with the touchpoints, and (5) identifying those touchpoints in need of improvement.

When firms are in the early stages of developing customer measures, it can be good to start with transactional measures and journey mapping. CPM analytics, however, is fundamentally about building and managing relationships and involves understanding what customers are likely to do going forward and why. The disadvantage of transactional measures is that they are less informative of what customers are likely to do in the future compared to more cumulative, overall evaluations of a customer's experience to date with a brand or company.[4] Customers' decisions are influenced by their entire history with a brand and not just their most recent visit to a theme park or their most recent flight on an airline. Cross-transactional measures (in this case, cumulative customer satisfaction) is a better indicator of future behavior—that is, customers' propensity to remain loyal, switch to a competitor, increase or decrease purchase volume, and pay higher or lower prices for a product or service. Put simply, cumulative customer satisfaction is a more forward-looking measure. It captures differences in the customer experience across competitors, as related to their innovativeness and superior value propositions, making it a better predictor. We thus focus on modeling cumulative customer satisfaction here.

As part of a management information system, satisfaction models provide direct insight into a brand's areas of competitive advantage to leverage, competitive vulnerabilities in need of improvement, basic or "must have" qualities to be maintained, and areas that require less attention. Three specific measures are required to provide these insights, keeping in mind that the drivers of satisfaction vary by relationship segment:

(1) Customer evaluations of how well a brand performs, both in an absolute sense and relative to competitors, on the qualities and costs that determine customer satisfaction.

(2) The statistical impact of these qualities and costs on customer satisfaction. More specifically, how much the variation in a particular product or service benefit, quality, or cost factor impacts customer satisfaction.

(3) The subsequent impact of improvements in customer satisfaction on business performance metrics of import to the brand (e.g., customer retention or churn; relationship leverage, as through share of wallet; relationship conversion; or customer acquisition, as through positive word of mouth).

Linking Quality, Satisfaction, and Business Performance

In this section we draw upon established methods to improve customer satisfaction, loyalty and profit. [5] Consider the simplified example of a satisfaction model in figure 6.1. In this case, customers experience varying levels of three generic brand qualities or benefits: product quality, service quality, and value or price. Each of these benefits are the result of a variety of more specific attributes, where service quality attributes may include the timeliness, accuracy, friendliness, and professionalism of the service experiences while product quality attributes may include the size, range, durability, reliability, and availability of the products. Value, as a measure of price, may be measured as the price paid given the quality received and price relative to competitors in the category. Surveys are used to measure these experiences as well as customers' overall satisfaction and loyalty intentions, while CRM systems provide measures of customers' behavior and business performance metrics over time.

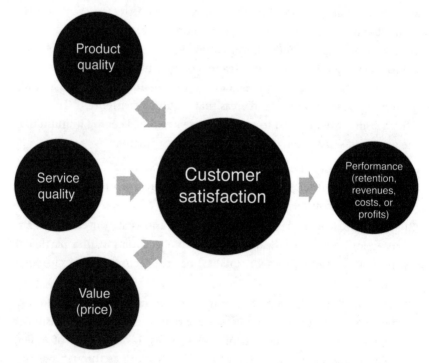

Figure 6.1
A generic customer satisfaction model.

Statistical modeling is used to determine how much the variance in product quality, service quality, and value across consumers in a relationship segment impact customer satisfaction, and the degree to which improvements in satisfaction impact subsequent performance metrics. The output of this modeling provides the information necessary to perform an *impact-performance analysis.* Qualities that have a high impact on satisfaction and demonstrate strong performance represent a brand's competitive advantages. Continuing to improve or maintain these "things gone right" helps build brand strength and convert customers to stronger relationships. Qualities found to have a high impact on satisfaction and weak performance are competitive vulnerabilities or weaknesses that require more immediate attention, lest customers defect. Fixing these "things gone wrong" plugs the leaks in the leaky bucket. High performance and low impact qualities, in contrast, can mean different things. In many cases they represent must-have qualities that customers expect, are consistently delivered, and are important to maintain—think Six Sigma quality, with respect to safety. In other cases, these qualities represent areas of product or service improvement that end up having little impact on customer satisfaction and resulting performance, where costs may be reduced.

The interpretation of low performance and low impact qualities depends on whether it involves qualities or price. If product or service qualities have low performance and impact, it simply means they are less consequential to customers and need not be improved. Price is different. If the goal is to compete on quality rather than price, the ideal would be for price to have low performance (i.e., a high price to the customer) but with little to no impact. Customers would essentially be telling the brand that its prices are high, but it doesn't matter since the qualities it provides make it worthwhile. In economic terms, if price has low impact and low performance, the brand excels at extracting "surplus" in the form of contribution margins from the customer.

A Tire Company Application

An application of satisfaction modeling in a B2B setting illustrates both the information that emerges from the analysis and the importance of interpreting the output.[6] The company in this case manufactures a full line of tire products for vehicles which it sells through its own franchised stores and independent retailers. To better understand how to improve customer satisfaction and business performance, the company commissioned a systematic study of the driving forces behind customer satisfaction and loyalty for replacement tires. The study focused on independent retailers' distribution channel, as most end users were found to purchase a tire brand based on the retailer's recommendation. From a CPM standpoint, the independent retailers represented friends in the manufacturer's relationship segmentation scheme—that is, regular, high-volume purchasers that fall short of a formal partnership, whereas franchised stores are more contractual partnerships. The tire company's goal was to increase cooperation with the independent retailers, converting some friendships into higher value partnerships.

The first step in the process was the use of qualitative interviews with retail customers to build the lens of the customer—that is, what are the more specific quality-related product and service attributes and benefits that drive customer satisfaction. The interviews used the *critical incident technique*, a method whereby customers describe specific likes and dislikes about their relationship with the company in order to build the customer lens.[7] Analysis of the qualitative interviews yielded the following benefit categories, with examples of the attributes used to measure each benefit:

1. **Tire Product**: Product quality, durability, range of sizes and types of tires for different vehicles.

2. **Pricing**: Price levels for different types of tires.

3. **Sales Department & Local Sales Representative**: The quality of cooperation with both the company's regional sales office and the retailer's local company representative.

4. **Shipping and Delivery**: The timing of deliveries, accuracy of shipments, and cooperation with the transport company.

5. **Discounts and Payments**: Aspects of pricing related to volume discounts, financing, and penalties for late payments.

6. **Sales Activities & Support**: The quality of company-sponsored sales activities and promotional materials, including tire stands, brochures, etc.

7. **Promotional Activities**: The quality of company-provided promotional activities, including vehicle rallies, hats, shirts, and other tchotchkes.

8. **Complaint Handling**: How well and how quickly retailer complaints are handled.

This customer lens was used as the template for a customer satisfaction survey that was administered to hundreds of the retail brand's tire dealers. Each dealer rated both the company and its primary competitor on all the attributes in each benefit category, overall (cumulative) customer satisfaction, and customer loyalty. Statistical modeling of the survey results provided the company with measures of the impact of each benefit category on customer satisfaction, the impact of satisfaction on loyalty, and the levels of performance on the benefits, satisfaction, and loyalty. Figure 6.2 shows the output of the benefit-level impact-performance analysis for both the company and its primary competitor.

The impact scores in this case indicate the degree to which improvement in each benefit category increases overall satisfaction (i.e., the beta coefficients from regression analysis). For example, an impact score of 0.30 predicts that a 10 percent increase in customer evaluations of a benefit increases overall satisfaction by 3 percent. The analysis also provides levels of performance for each of the benefit categories. The individual attributes for each benefit were rated on a scale of 1–10 (from poor to excellent) and each benefit was measured as a weighted index of its attributes (based on the statistical modeling). The 1–10-point weighted indices were transformed into a 0–100-point performance score for presentation purposes.

The management task is to evaluate the output of the impact-performance analysis and develop strategic priorities for the tire company with respect to its friends. More specifically, what areas are the highest priority for improvement, be they weaknesses that will lead to defections or strengths to be improved and leveraged to convert customers to closer relationships?

Interpreting the Output

Data analytics, of course, only inform decisions rather than make them. Managers and executives must interpret the output to make business decisions. Impact and performance should be evaluated both in an absolute sense—that is, what is possible—and relative to competitors. If product or service quality shows significant impact and moderate performance, while competitors show weak performance, it may be a competitive advantage

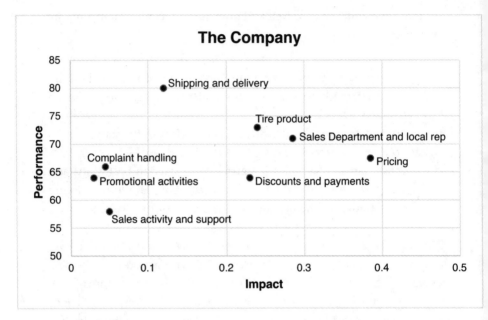

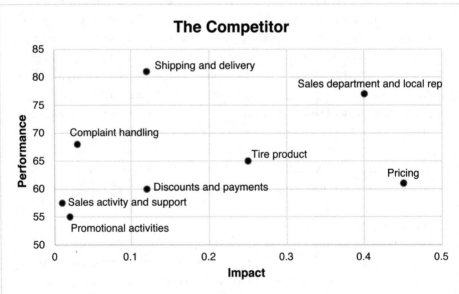

Figure 6.2
Impact-performance analysis for the tire company and primary competitor

in the near term but show room for improvement in the longer term. The information should also be evaluated relative to a brand's strategy, as related to our discussion of product or service qualities versus price. If the strategy is to compete on quality, then perceived price or value is one area where lower impact and lower performance (i.e., higher prices) may be desirable.

In the tire company example, all these considerations come into play. Both the company's and the competitor's impact-performance charts show complaint handling, promotional activities, and sales activities and support having low impact and weaker performance. These are areas where the company is unlikely to gain significant ROI. Shipping and delivery show high performance but only moderately higher impact for both companies. The interpretation here is likely that shipping and delivery is a basic or must-have quality, meaning it is reliably provided with relatively little variance. While it is important to maintain performance on this benefit, it is not necessarily a competitive advantage or competitive vulnerability.

The other four benefit categories have higher impact and are where the management team should focus. Classifying these benefit categories as strengths or weaknesses depends both on absolute impact and performance (the company's chart) and relative impact and performance (comparison to the competitor's chart). The company's performance on tire product is higher than the competitor with relatively equal impact. In the near term, tire product is a relative strength. The company's sales department and local rep, however, is a relative weakness when compared to the competitor. Discounts and payments may be an absolute weakness (moderate impact, low performance), but it is a relative strength versus the competitor. Finally, pricing (remember that higher performance on price means more attractive, or lower, prices) is another relative strength (high impact, higher relative performance), meaning that the company need not compete more on price in the short term.

The question with respect to pricing, however, is how much does the company really want to compete on price? Creating closer partnerships in a customer portfolio over time requires decreasing the focus on price by increasing differentiation and customization on nonprice attributes and benefits. Thus, the strategy with the greatest ROI in this case may be to continuously improve tire product (e.g., dealer-specific tire sizes and types), sales department and local rep (e.g., customized ordering systems and dedicated sales rep), and discounts and payments (e.g., compete more on quality and indirectly on price, as through financing terms and volume discounts). Through this process, the company will turn more friends into partners.

Impacts on Business Performance

With respect to the impact of satisfaction on firm performance, meaningful measures vary from industry to industry, brand to brand, and relationship segment to relationship segment. Performance metrics range from actual customer churn to purchase volume or revenues to costs to profitability. In the case of our tire manufacturer, increasing the satisfaction of independent tire retailers will encourage the retailers to carry a larger inventory and range of tires and make them more likely to recommend the manufacturer's tires to end users. By linking quality improvements at the attribute and benefit levels to satisfaction, and satisfaction to subsequent business performance, it becomes possible to predict the value of those improvements. Note that the frequency of this type of analysis depends on how quickly, or slowly, the market is changing. The more dynamic the market, the more frequent the analysis as customer needs and competitive offerings evolve.

Another important advantage of statistical estimates is that they tell when enough is enough. That is, when is there an ROI and when isn't there? The principle here is that improving customer satisfaction is not a maximization problem, but rather an optimization problem. At some point, increasing satisfaction has diminishing returns and even negative returns, where the cost of continued improvements in customer satisfaction outweighs the benefits. The optimal level of satisfaction varies by customer and market segment.

Consider the example of a brand of limited-service hotels, where the value of relationship investments through customer satisfaction is predicated on whether continued improvements in satisfaction generate additional hotel revenues (RevPAR, or revenue per available room).[8] Improvements in the brand's qualities and customer satisfaction have very positive impacts on revenue generation for some properties in the chain but not others. Satisfaction is more likely to improve RevPAR for properties located in cities, near airports, and in leisure (vacation) destinations, while the impact on properties in rural, small market, and suburban areas is negligible. This difference is due to the fact that different locations cater to very different market segments. The business and vacation travelers who frequent urban, airport, and vacation properties are more likely to return to those locations as repeat customers (friends or partners) and have choices. Further investments in satisfaction and relationship strength allow these properties to compete for future revenue streams. When dissatisfied, these customers have options in competing brands. In contrast, the transient customers who frequent rural, small market, and suburban properties are more likely to be infrequent customers (acquaintances) who are "just passing through." The prospect of future revenues is limited with fewer choices, meaning that investments in satisfaction and retention have a lower ROI.

Using all the information in statistical impact modeling to make resource allocation decisions and drive product and process change is the key to building strong brands and relationship strength. It is the basis for improving a brand's competitive advantages when acquiring new customers or converting them to stronger relationships, and eliminating competitive vulnerabilities to improve retention. We recognize that, in some cases, statistical estimates of impact may not be possible, such as when sample sizes are small. An alternative is to rely on self-rated importance measures (e.g., how important is this quality on a scale from 1 "not at all important" to 10 "very important"?) as a substitute for an impact-performance analysis. Where possible, however, statistically derived impact scores are more diagnostic and informative.[9]

But even the best measurement systems and metrics lose their value when they become compromised in an organization. We have seen this happen at the point of sale when salespeople coach customers to give them high performance scores ("Make sure you give me all 10s on our survey!") or more sensitive metrics are replaced by simpler ones, such as top-box scores (i.e., the percentage of customers in the top boxes of a measurement scale) or net promoter scores (i.e., the percentage of customers who promote the brand less the percentage of detractors). Combining customers into those who, for example, score 8–10 on a 10-point performance scale into one performance category ("satisfied customers") when most customers fall in that range may make a company or business unit look better, but it removes the very information needed to pinpoint the root causes of customer defections and relationship conversion. Information systems that allow salespeople or service providers to encourage higher ratings also mitigate or reduce variance in the measures, effectively transforming systems designed to identify root causes into service response systems with limited variance and strategic value.

A lack of alignment across business divisions further compromises the value of customer information systems. The root causes of relationship conversion and customer defection require organization-wide product and process change, not just feel-good responses from customer response teams that are disconnected from other divisions. We find that this alignment around customers comes more naturally to smaller companies and start-ups, where customers are visible and important to all members in the organization as a kind of collective responsibility. Customer expectations are not only fulfilled but enhanced as the start-up is keen to learn directly from customers how to improve its products and services. As a company grows, competitors copy its success and create their own differentiation. Growth leads companies to organize their resources more around internal activities and functions, such as procurement, production, distribution, and sales, rather than customer relationships. This limits the ability of information systems to help create a more profitable customer portfolio.

Chapter Summary

CPM analytics and statistical impact modeling help close the gap between the customer experience that executives believe they provide and what their companies actually provide. It requires understanding the difference between transaction-specific measures of the experience, measures that facilitate process design, and cumulative or cross-transactional measures that are better predictors of customer behavior and resulting business performance. The modeling of customer satisfaction, where product and service qualities are linked to satisfaction and satisfaction is linked to business performance, is fundamental to CPM. Here the use of transactional measures is no substitute for cumulative measures of satisfaction and may actually lead companies to focus on the wrong priorities. By estimating both the impact and performance of the qualities and costs that drive customer satisfaction, these predictive models identify competitive advantages, disadvantages, and vulnerabilities, and the basic qualities that customers have come to expect.

An important takeaway from this chapter is that the outputs of satisfaction modeling link directly to the core management decisions of CPM. Competitive advantages, those qualities of high impact and high performance, are areas to be leveraged in customer acquisition and relationship conversion. Competitive disadvantages are areas of competitive vulnerability in need of improvement that are essential to relationship defense. Addressing these vulnerabilities plugs holes in the large leaky bucket of customers. Another takeaway is the importance of building these models on a relationship segmentation scheme. In applications of CPM, acquaintances are more likely impacted by price, availability, and convenience, friends by product or service quality and the brand itself, and partners by the attractions of customization and adaptation to a brand's ecosystem and community.

The metrics, of course, only inform management decisions; they do not make those decisions. Managers and executives must decide on the CPM goals related to customer acquisition, relationship defense, relationship leverage, and relationship conversion. But even the best CPM analytics and metrics may be compromised by focusing on simple measures or lacking organizational alignment. A large, international chemicals company developed both a strong CPM relationship segmentation scheme of acquaintances, friends, and partners and a sophisticated predictive modeling capability applied to those segments. It used these capabilities to develop unique strategies for each segment but failed to reach the full benefit due to a lack of organizational alignment. We return to this issue of organizational alignment in chapter 7, where we also take up the question, "what is marketing management anyway?"

7   Capturing Value through CPM

In the late nineteenth century, retail entrepreneur John Wanamaker is credited with saying that "half my advertising spend is wasted; the trouble is, I don't know which half."[1] In those days, companies did not have the tools and frameworks required to understand where the money would be better spent. Firms benefit today from decades of research into and applications of marketing research, tools that include satisfaction modeling, customer lifetime value calculations, the CPM framework, and CPM analytics. These tools and frameworks exist to improve the ROI of market-related activities. But our experience is that most companies don't use them. They may have invested in information technology and data scientists, but they have not necessarily organized these capabilities effectively. A customer-centric organization understands how to organize its capabilities and leverage its analytics to create value across all the relationships in a portfolio. This means being more effective, or doing the right things, and more efficient, or doing things in the right way. Here in chapter 7, we comment on the role of top management in *CPM value creation*, the more specific role of the marketing function, and an evolving approach to market management that is adaptable to both brand portfolios and relationship segments.

But before we proceed, we return to one of the more important lessons from creating a large leaky bucket of customers—that is, to avoid myopic strategies, and specifically to avoid a narrow interpretation of *customer centricity*. The concept is easily lost in translation. Put simply, customer centricity holds that because the lifetime value of individual customers is very different, companies are better off focusing on high value customers.[2] This principle is embedded in the importance of relationship conversion within our framework. The problem is that customer centricity can be interpreted narrowly as a need to focus on friends and partners to the exclusion of strangers and acquaintances. This ignores the long-term value of adding weaker relationships to a portfolio, as a customer's current value is not the same as their future value. A major tenet of CPM is that while closer, more profitable customer relationships are indeed more valuable, loyalty is fleeting, and weaker relationships are a primary source for future loyal customers. Interpreted within the framework of CPM, a customer-centric organization creates value through both the stronger and weaker relationships in a portfolio.

Top Management

As a framework that balances competing priorities in a firm, a CPM approach to decision making must come from the top. We have found it essential that top management be involved in the process. Top management teams espouse the importance of maximizing shareholder value but do not necessarily make customers and their downstream revenues a priority toward achieving that goal.[3] As we saw in chapter 6, understanding what drives customer satisfaction informs the decisions related to achieving CPM-related goals.

In the framework of CPM, top management should decide how and how much to invest in customer acquisition, relationship defense, relationship conversion, and relationship leverage. In practice, however, top management teams rarely involve themselves in these decisions. Rather, they focus on products, production, and organizational issues rather than customers. As CPM analytics inform these decisions, top management should incorporate this information into decisions regarding organizational structures, systems, and procedures for coordination. Monitoring business performance on key performance indicators (KPIs) is central to management control, and CPM analytics can provide the KPIs needed to grow and protect the portfolio. With a strategy that includes explicit targets for acquaintances, friends, and partners, monitoring the size of each relationship segment and its share of a portfolio are key indicators of performance. If there are not enough new customers entering the portfolio, or there is an increase in customer defections, the management team can take corrective action. CPM analytics and customer satisfaction modeling give top managers information they ordinarily would not obtain from traditional management information systems. Satisfaction modeling, as it underscores a firm's competitive advantages and vulnerabilities, is essential as top management seeks to close the gap between what executives believe they do for customers and how they actually perform. The reality is, however, that many top management teams seldom use these tools.

The Marketing Function

Marketing should be an organization-wide set of activities that connects customers to the company through branded products and services. Yet the marketing function is often narrowly understood as a set of communication activities attempting to create awareness and sales. This includes advertising, email marketing, and personal sales calls. We return to this question of "what is marketing anyway?" later in the chapter. That said, a common objective of advertising is to increase sales by attracting new customers and retaining existing customers. But traditional marketing and management information systems usually do not inform managers about the number of new customers versus retained customers in a portfolio, making it impossible to assess the effects of activities such as advertising. To analyze the effect of marketing interventions, companies need to break down sales into those from strangers, acquaintances, friends, and partners. They need to develop new management information systems with relevant, portfolio-based metrics in place, most importantly a time series of new customers, retained customers, and relationship segment size. This allows companies not only to document the effect of marketing investments but to dig deeper into the effectiveness of those investments across relationship segments. Assessing the ROI of marketing activities becomes an achievable goal.

The value of email marketing is one example, where the goal is twofold. One is to increase sales by motivating existing customers to purchase more, as through more frequent purchases, purchasing additional products or services, or extending the life of the relationship. The second is to motivate estranged or former customers to reengage with the brand or company. Amazon's email interventions are often aimed at these two goals. CPM analytics are needed to keep track of and document the effect of the email interventions on existing customers and on winning back estranged customers. Analytics allow companies to investigate how variation in subject lines and variation in email content (text and pictures) affect opening, clicks, and conversion to sales rates for different relationship segments. With these analytical tools companies can leverage their investments in email marketing systems and staff.

Personal selling is an important marketing tool in most B2B markets but also in many B2C markets such as vehicles and financial services. As with advertising and emails, the primary objective of a sale is two-fold. One is to acquire new customers, and the second is to strengthen and leverage existing customer relationships. CPM analytics can assist the sales organization in identifying prospects with high potential and equip sales representatives with important information about their prospects. A customer's potential may be calculated through solid statistical methods and machine learning, which may be updated dynamically as new information is registered in various data sources. CPM analytics assist the sales organization with respect to the timing and purpose of sales contacts with existing customers. Calls on existing customers may be supported from a centralized sales office assisting with emails and meeting schedules. Personal selling becomes more effective and more efficient, more effective because the sales calls are better aligned with customer needs and preferences, and more efficient because the time the sales organization traditionally has spent on information gathering and planning is now in the database.

As connecting with customers is an organization-wide set of activities, other business functions are involved in developing customer portfolio growth. Recall the success of Sector Alarm, which took a problem with an alarm system and turned it into stronger customer relationships through a coordinated, cross-functional solution. Within the framework of CPM, product managers gain information on product usage and satisfaction across different segments of customers and use the information to make sure that their products are attractive and valuable. Operations obtain transactional information on how satisfied customers are across their network of stores and other facilities where customers interact with the brand and the company. Likewise, R&D obtains more insight into customer needs and what product and service innovations will attract customers in different relationship segments, eliminate competitive vulnerabilities, and build competitive advantage.

What is Marketing Management Anyway?

Our typology of relationship segments rests on the strength of a customer's relationship with a company or a brand, which in turn is based on a value proposition, be that parity value, differential value, or customized value. Portfolio management's use of relationship strength and value propositions as the primary basis for market segmentation raises a fundamental question—what is marketing management anyway? How we teach marketing management has remained relatively unchanged for decades. In traditional market management and segmentation, the focus is on customer needs as a basis for strategic market planning. The identification of underserved, needs-based segments drives target market, product, and positioning strategies and related marketing mix decisions (pricing, promotion, and distribution) to maximize sales and product profitability. Pioneering firms such as Procter & Gamble recognized the limitations of mass marketing and found that focusing on subgroups of customers with similar needs and wants produced a competitive advantage, increased revenues, and lowered costs per customer. Needs-based segmentation rests on understanding just what problem or problems the customer is trying to solve and the experience they are trying to achieve. In his classic article "Marketing Myopia," Ted Levitt made the point that companies fail because they think of their businesses too narrowly and ignore what the customer is trying to achieve.[4] Railroad companies failed because they considered themselves to be in the railroad business, not the transportation business. Sports teams are successful because they understand they are in the entertainment business, not just the sports business.

The value of needs-based segmentation is that it captures layers of customer heterogeneity, from macrosegments to microsegments, which map into value propositions that can be stable over time. Underneath the macrosegments are more layered microsegments that differentiate customers in important ways, including demographic, geographic, and psychographic (e.g., lifestyle, personality) segments, and actual behavior (e.g., heavy versus light users). Individual products or brands and their value propositions are then tailored to the segments. Marriott, for example, has a segmentation scheme for all 30 brands in its portfolio.[5] It categorizes brands into six macrosegments based on three levels of quality and corresponding price point desired, from select-service properties to premium properties to luxury properties, and whether customers seek a more traditional, "classic" hotel experience or a more "distinctive" experience based on hotel design, amenities, and cuisine. Whereas Ritz-Carlton is a classic luxury brand, Bulgari is a distinctive luxury brand, each targeted at a selective population of affluent customers. Courtyard by Marriott is a classic select-service brand targeted at business travelers, while AC Hotels is a distinctive select-service brand featuring a distinctive European design with limited amenities targeted at younger customers at a lower price point.

But the CPM framework requires a broader perspective. Needs-based segmentation competes with other priorities in a firm, most importantly unit costs and economies of scale. This leads to a very different view where marketing, or being market-based, is a focus rather than a function. As Peter Drucker said decades ago:

> Marketing is so basic that is cannot be considered a separate function . . . It is the whole business seen from the point of view of its final results, that is, from the customer's point of view. Concern and responsibility for marketing must therefore permeate all areas of the enterprise.[6]

Drucker points out that a true customer and market orientation is an organization-wide process that impacts a firm's strategy, the disposition of its employees, and its customers' attitudes and behaviors.[7] It requires a focus on customers, competitors, costs, and interorganizational coordination beyond the boundaries of traditional marketing and brand management. Whether relative commodities or differentiated offerings are involved, firms that dedicate themselves to a true market orientation see a positive impact on business performance.[8] We see this broader perspective of marketing—that is, taking a market orientation—as very consistent with our CPM framework.

The Customer Portfolio–Product Portfolio Market Matrix

Needs-based segmentation remains an important part of marketing and CPM. As we have argued, however, customer behavior is dynamic. Customers simultaneously operate in multiple needs-based segments depending on the context. How do we then reconcile CPM with traditional market segmentation? An emergent framework is to view marketing management as the intersection of customer portfolio management, product portfolio management, and brand management.[9]

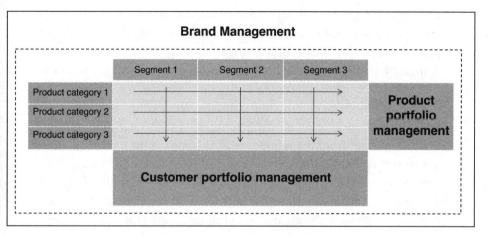

Figure 7.1
Marketing management as a product portfolio–segment portfolio market matrix.

Figure 7.1 illustrates this market matrix approach, where CPM manages revenues and profits based on a portfolio of customer segments and product categories. Brands are used both at a product category level (i.e., Ritz-Carlton, Courtyard, etc.) and at a company level (i.e., Marriott, Marriott Bonvoy). Applying the framework to the Marriott example, customer segments may include target customers (strangers) and all six levels of the Bonvoy loyalty program, recognizing that those levels map into three underlying relationship segments (acquaintances, friends, and partners). The product brands would include all 30 Marriott brands categorized into their six macro market segments (classic luxury, distinctive luxury, classic premium, distinctive premium, classic select, and distinctive select). Needs-based segmentation is not lost in the framework, as the cells in the market matrix should reflect the fit between brands, or categories of brands, and the needs of the relationship segment.

The advantage of this approach is that the market matrix recognizes that relationship segments "fit" multiple brands or needs-based segments depending on the use occasion or context. Managers can put values in the cells that reflect the strength of the fit, for example weak (0), moderate (+), or strong (++) for each brand–relationship combination. Once populated, a brand–relationship matrix provides a roadmap for customer acquisition, relationship defense, relationship leverage, and relationship conversion. In this way, the matrix highlights which brands to market to which relationship segments. Readers familiar with *quality function deployment* (QFD), a well-established quality improvement method, and its "house of quality" will see parallels with this matrix approach.[10] Whereas the house of quality translates customer needs and wants (the voice of the customer) into design and engineering characteristics (the voice of the engineer), the brand–relationship market matrix translates relationship segments into applicable macrosegments, microsegments, and brand-value propositions.

What emerges from the framework is an approach to marketing management that emphasizes customer acquisition, defense, leverage, and conversion as four essential and connected strategies. The strategic market planning process remains intact with its focus on assessing market attractiveness, competitors, threats and opportunities, setting financial goals and budgets, and the implementation of brand strategies. As the brand (product) portfolio grows and relationships emerge, the market matrix makes it easier to see the connections between the "whats" in the matrix (the relationship segments and what they prefer) and the "hows" (the brand-value propositions that are most likely to meet or exceed expectations, increase satisfaction, build relationships, and retain customers). The strategic market planning process and matrix development require analytical support to track customer and business performance metrics, understand competitive advantages and vulnerabilities, and maximize effectiveness (ROI).

Market Share versus Customer Satisfaction

The market matrix approach stands to address another central question in marketing management—that is, should a brand focus on increasing market share or customer satisfaction? We have emphasized the importance of simultaneously pursuing both offensive and defensive strategies within the framework of CPM, offense to add new customers to a portfolio and defense to limit defections and increase profit per customer through higher customer satisfaction, understanding that both strategies effectively increase the size of a portfolio. But the relationship between market share gains and increases in satisfaction is itself dynamic. Earlier marketing research suggested that gains in market share and satisfaction were not necessarily compatible goals, the reason being that a larger market share requires a particular brand to serve an increasingly heterogeneous population of customers.[11] Subsequent research has taken a closer look at the effects of both market share gains on satisfaction and satisfaction gains on market share.[12] Market share gains do indeed result in lower satisfaction as a brand appeals to a more heterogeneous customer population. At the same time, increasing satisfaction increases market share over time. This occurs when a brand's satisfaction exceeds competitors' brand satisfaction and switching costs are low.

These seemingly contradictory results can be explained by the need for brand proliferation as market share grows. The negative effect of market share gains on satisfaction is alleviated when a firm grows its portfolio of sub-brands. As market share grows and customer demand is more heterogeneous, customer satisfaction can be maintained through the launch of multiple brands or sub-brands to a growing range of needs-based market segments. Within the emergent market matrix approach in figure 7.1, declining satisfaction in a relationship segment may signal the need for further brand development. With the digitalization of customer interactions, where brand communications involve both mass communication (the same message to all customers) and customized communications (e.g., email, apps, individualized customer service), brands may be differentiated or customized at a finer level, thus facilitating micro-segmentation. Traditional brand positioning theory, focused on the average customer, focuses on macro-segmentation simply because the communication method was mass advertising.

As it directly impacts both current and future cash flows, the market matrix should be analyzed and monitored at the highest levels of an organization. This task goes beyond the boundaries of marketing to include finance and overall corporate strategy. The challenge is to translate the matrix into an organizational structure with clear management objectives and roles. Ultimately it is the responsibility of the CEO to make sure that the company maintains an appropriate focus on customer relationship segments, invests in a brand portfolio needed to compete for those customers, and creates an organizational structure to compete effectively and efficiently. One company we know operated in three distinct B2B product categories that involved the same customers and relationship segments but completely different sales and delivery organizations. The relationship segments were managed independent of sales and delivery resulting in significant inefficiencies. In smaller and medium-sized companies, sales and delivery are more likely to be integrated and directly involve the CEO or president, especially when partners or friends are involved. No matter how large an organization becomes, staying close to customers is a lesson that large firms should continue to learn from smaller ones. As Herb Kelleher, the longtime head of Southwest Airlines once said, "Think small and act small, and we'll get bigger. Think big and act big, and we'll get smaller."[13]

Chapter Summary

Through an emphasis on balancing both offensive and defensive market strategies, CPM seeks to avoid myopic strategies that focus too singularly on a brand's highest value customers or a blind pursuit of short-term volume. By considering both the need for cost leadership and differentiation, market share and customer satisfaction become compatible goals. The clear takeaway is the need for top management to own the customer portfolio, its strategy, and the investment decisions that follow. Management goals should include deciding how much to spend and organize around acquiring new customers, moving a subset of customers to closer, more profitable relationships, leveraging these relationships through a larger portfolio of product and service brands, and defending relationships through improvements in customer satisfaction and higher switching costs.

Creating value through CPM also suggests that we take a new look at how marketing management has evolved. Building on its traditional focus on needs-based segmentation, a more dynamic approach to marketing maps relationship segments into brand-value propositions that evolve over time as customer relationships grow. The result is a roadmap for companies as they develop and improve value propositions, convert customers from weaker to stronger relationships, and grow CPLV. In our eighth and final chapter we turn to the simple question of where to start the process of customer portfolio management. We return to the basic framework of CPM, review what we have learned, and explore how digitalization and the growth of digital platforms and omnichannel marketing provides answers.

8   Getting Started with CPM: A Roadmap

Managers and executives may find the management of an entire portfolio of customers, products, and brands to be a daunting task. Further complicating the task are major innovations and resulting disruptions to our economy. Many businesses are still adapting to the development of digital product and service platforms. Add the evolution of machine learning and AI, and the task may appear insurmountable. There is a path to developing a CPM strategy while embracing these changes. Here in our closing chapter, we review the basic takeaways from previous chapters and focus on where to get started, with a discussion of how digitalization can help to jump-start a company's CPM strategy.

A Review of CPM: Start with Segmentation

Recall that customer portfolio management emerged as a concept as we observed firms struggling with competing business priorities. After decades of focusing on sales and market share as keys to marketing and business performance, the emphasis shifted from offense to defense. Customer satisfaction and retention emerged as priorities, underscoring the value of creating strong relationships with customers. This led companies to focus, in some cases myopically, on customer retention and profit per customer in the form of customer lifetime value. The problem with that approach was that the need for offensive marketing didn't just go away—adding new customers to a portfolio and maintaining economies of scale remain important goals. As the old business adage goes, companies either grow or die.

Our metaphor of the value of a large leaky bucket captures these competing priorities, where the goal is to create a bucket of customers that includes both leaky or weaker customer relationships and more watertight or stronger relationships. While the stronger relationships create greater value today, the weaker relationships are an investment in the future. Plugging leaks in the bucket, as through improved quality and customer satisfaction to retain closer and more profitable customers, is a key to increasing profit per customer and capturing future revenue streams. But a singular focus on loyal customers is unsustainable. Even your most loyal customers eventually leave, making it equally important to constantly add new customers to the portfolio. These customers provide both scale and a source of future loyal customers.

The framework of CPM (see figure 2.1) is the best place to start in developing a CPM strategy. But even that assumes top management buy in, which is by no means a given. With top management on board, the process begins with the development of a market segmentation scheme based on the benefits created and the strength of the relationships that customers have with a brand, company, or organization. We have found segmenting customers into strangers, acquaintances, friends, and partners to be a robust approach to relationship segmentation. Strangers are prospective customers who have little to no familiarity with or awareness of a brand, but also include former customers who no longer purchase the brand. Acquaintances have a parity relationship with a brand, a relationship based more on price, availability, and convenience than on differentiation. Friends perceive a brand as differentiated, with higher quality making it attractive even at a higher price. Finally, partnerships involve more customized offerings where customers are embedded in a brand's ecosystem of products, services, and brand communities on a continuous basis.

Although relationship segmentation that includes true partnerships is intuitive in a B2B context, it has become more common in a B2C context in recent years through the development of digital platforms, customer loyalty programs and brand communities. Our case example in chapter 2 of a building materials retailer underscored the value of this first important step, where segmenting current customers into acquaintances, friends, and partners based on brand preference and share of wallet revealed huge differences across stores in the chain. While more profitable stores had a high percentage of friends and partners, low performing stores had predominantly acquaintance customers. The brand was able to increase profitability across the chain by sharing best practices from high performing to low performing stores and converting some acquaintances to friends and some friends to partners.

The second step in the framework is to better understand the lifetime value of each relationship segment. Prescriptively, this requires a closer consideration of both scale economies and customer heterogeneity, where customer heterogeneity translates into opportunities to pursue brand differentiation and customization strategies. From a business strategy standpoint, cost leadership, differentiation, and customization all play vital roles in CPM. Our CPLV model provides general guidelines or prescriptions regarding when and how much to focus on weaker customer relationships as through sales volume and market share, versus stronger customer relationships as through a focus on quality improvement, customer satisfaction, and retention. These prescriptions include:

1. In more commodity markets where weaker customer relationships dominate (homogeneous demand), the focus is naturally on a volume-based strategy and cost leadership.

2. As customer heterogeneity grows, where brands can create an advantage through product or service differentiation and customization, the value of creating friends and partners grows with it. Our simulations of CPLV to date suggest that cost leadership (economies of scale) and the creation of stronger customer relationships (through adaptation to customer heterogeneity) have roughly equal long-term impact on CPLV.

3. As most markets include both significant scale economies *and* customer heterogeneity, balancing offensive and defensive marketing activities is essential to the long-term profitability of a customer portfolio, underscoring the value of a large leaky bucket of customers.

4. Whether in relatively stable or more turbulent market environments, a strategy focused on creating a competitive advantage with respect to relationship defense is particularly effective. A defensive strategy leverages both scale economies through customer retention and higher margins from closer customer relationships.

With a foundational relationship segmentation scheme and a general understanding of the value of offensive and defensive strategies in hand, the third major stage of CPM is goal setting. This involves boiling the complexities of CPM down to four key strategic questions: (1) how much to invest in customer acquisition, (2) how much to invest in defending existing customer relationships, (3) how to leverage existing relationships, as through purchase volume or the cross-selling of products and services across a larger brand ecosystem, and (4) how to convert weaker relationships into stronger, more profitable relationships. In chapter 3 we provided examples of relationship acquisition, defense, leverage, and conversion as they apply to different relationship segments. That said, few firms systematically develop all four goals for all relationship segments, where firms like Amazon are an exception.

Closing the gap between where you are and where you need to be with respect to these strategic questions requires building capabilities related to CPM analytics. We break this process down into three workflows: (1) the development of a customer database built upon relationship segments, (2) developing an understanding of the causal relationships in this data, and (3) the development of predictive scoring models of how customers are likely to respond to market-related activities. An effective customer database focuses on smart or informative variables from different data sources that embrace the variability inherent in customers' perceptions, experiences, and behaviors. With respect to causality, decades of customer and marketing research have taught us the central importance of a particular causal link. This is the link from customer perceptions of brand quality and cost to overall evaluations of customer satisfaction to the positive impacts of satisfaction on business performance and the market value of a firm.

This means that modeling the impact of quality and cost perceptions on customer satisfaction provides the information required to make resource allocation decisions across relationship segments. This includes where to focus quality improvements and innovation activities to defend and build customer relationships and how those activities impact business performance. Impact-performance analysis, which has become common in satisfaction research, provides the metrics required to balance the offensive and defensive marketing strategies that are essential to growing a customer portfolio. Defensively, when scoring models identify drivers of satisfaction that have high impact and weak performance, addressing those vulnerabilities prevents customers from exiting a portfolio. When satisfaction drivers have high impact and high performance, the scoring models identify areas that drive customer acquisition and relationship conversion.

Jump-Start the Process through Digitalization

Traditional business strategy often required a choice: to pursue cost leadership through economies of scale or to pursue differentiation in a subset of the market. The development of an effective, online digital platform for sales and service stands to foster a firm's ability to achieve both scale economies and differentiation, effectively jump-starting the CPM process. Our study of Amazon is a case in point. Through its development of a best-in-class online sales system and growing ecosystem of product and service categories, Amazon is constantly adding new customers to its portfolio, creating closer relationships through Amazon Prime, leveraging those relationships through cross-selling, and defending relationships through the delivery of high customer satisfaction. Amazon's digital platform allows it to achieve both economies of scale through technology and price premiums through differentiation. The point is simply that digitalization facilitates both cost leadership and differentiation, where firms avoid being caught between potentially inconsistent strategies.

Digitalization is also changing the ways that firms work with each other. In the B2C space, digitalization is fueling partnerships where customers are increasingly adapted to, and connected with, a network of brands and other customers. This creates a network effect, where the demand for a product or service increases as more people use it.[1] The value of a network increases as more people join, which in turn makes it more difficult for users to switch to a different network. As a result, the demand for the product or service becomes less elastic, meaning that the price can be increased without significantly reducing the number of users. The network effect can be seen in the case of operating systems such as Windows and macOS. The more people who use these operating systems, the more software developers create applications for them, which in turn makes them more valuable to users. This makes it difficult for users to switch to a different operating system, even if the price were to increase.

The result is a first-mover advantage in the digitalization of customer interactions.[2] Through digitalization companies become more connected with their customers, which leads to stronger value propositions, customer satisfaction, and a willingness to expand the relationship into more and more product categories. Price premiums and margins increase, and the costs for customers to switch from one digital platform to another will be higher than the traditional costs of switching from one brand to another. The competitive dynamics are such that there will be winners and losers in this race. The winners will emulate Amazon's success, while others will need to be creative with new formats of collaboration involving multiple companies from different product and service categories.

Companies will need to develop new strategies for customer acquisition, where mergers and acquisitions (M&A) are an option when regulations allow. In our study of hotels, Marriott and Hilton have built significant competitive advantage through a combination of M&A, or a larger portfolio of brands, and the development of improved digital platforms and collaborations in their loyalty programs, leaving other hotel competitors scrambling to catch up.[3] Another option is the formation of partner networks, where companies develop shared market platforms, such as a loyalty program platform shared by multiple companies. In this scenario, firms develop their own communication channels, but they share logistical services and benefits. In the lodging space, for example, Airbnb is making up for the lack of an in-platform loyalty program by partnering with other rewards programs like those from credit card companies and airlines.[4]

Develop a Roadmap

Taken together, our framework and the case studies used to illustrate it suggest a roadmap for getting started with CPM:

1. Get to know your customers better, especially if you haven't spent much time with them lately. Develop a relationship segmentation scheme for existing customers based on acquaintances, friends, and partners. And don't forget strangers and estranged customers who may be future customers.

2. Take concrete steps to improve customer acquisition and retention activities. Who in your organization is good at creating new customer accounts, who excels at keeping existing accounts, and what can you learn from them and share across the organization?

3. Take account of your analytical capabilities and how well they are leveraged in the organization. Using CPM analytics as a framework, ask yourself, how strong is your customer database, how well do you understand

causality or what drives customer behavior and resulting business performance, and have you developed the capability to predict what customers will do going forward?

4. Ask how your digital strategy can help jump-start the need to balance both growth and profitability.

5. Finally, constantly monitor your performance, and your competitors' performance, from the customers' perspective. What do acquaintances, friends, and partners see as your competitive advantages to be leveraged and competitive vulnerabilities that need attention?

Concluding Comments

We started our journey into customer portfolio management by asking the question of what a US telecom company and a Norwegian farm fishing company had in common. The lesson was that they were both effectively managing the complexities of a customer portfolio, the telecom company by understanding the need to balance both weaker and stronger relationships to maintain scale, and the fish farming company by developing brand value propositions tailored to different relationship segments. Our applications of CPM over the past 20 years have taught us a couple of simple rules. Get top management buy-in from the start regarding the importance of customers. It is hardly a surprise that Jeff Bezos and the folks at Amazon are obsessed with customers as the root of their success. If you are new to CPM, start small and build from there. The simple step of understanding who the acquaintances, friends, and partners are in your customer portfolio, as well as who the strangers are who are prospective customers, goes a long way toward providing the insight needed to improve performance. For a firm like Pan Fish, the fish farming company, this required development of a customized solution for true partners. For hotel companies like Marriott, this required a business strategy that made sure customers have all the brands they need in Marriott's brand portfolio and a loyalty program that tailors brand value propositions to relationship segments. For a company like Sector Alarm, portfolio management allowed it to turn a problem that would have led to customer defections into a cross-functional solution that created higher customer satisfaction and stronger, more profitable relationships.

Our business applications continue to reinforce the value of the CPM framework and the concept of customer portfolio lifetime value toward improving long-term business performance. We believe that the lessons learned along the way will help as you embark on your own customer portfolio management journey. If we leave you with any one thought, it is the value of maintaining a large leaky bucket of customers. This means balancing the need for both weaker and stronger relationships in a portfolio and balancing the offensive and defensive marketing strategies and investments that follow. It means avoiding a myopic focus on one strategy or the other. A myopic focus on weaker relationships will only leave money on the table, while a myopic focus on high-value customers will lead to a smaller and smaller portfolio over time. While customer loyalty is profitable, it is also fleeting.

Notes

Chapter 1

1. Fred Selnes and Michael D. Johnson, "Manage Your Customer Portfolio for Maximum Lifetime Value," *MIT Sloan Management Review* 64, no. 1 (2022): 22–27.

2. Claes Fornell, Michael D. Johnson, Eugene W. Anderson, Jaesung Cha, and Barbara Everitt Bryant, "The American Customer Satisfaction Index: Nature, Purpose, and Findings," *Journal of Marketing* 60, no. 4 (October 1996): 7–18, https://doi.org/10.2307/1251898.

3. Fornell et al.; Eugene W. Anderson, Claes Fornell, and Donald R. Lehmann, "Customer Satisfaction, Market Share, and Profitability: Findings from Sweden," *Journal of Marketing* 58, no. 3 (July 1994): 53–66, https://doi.org/10.1177/002224299405800304. Lopo L. Rego, Neil A. Morgan, and Claes Fornell, "Reexamining the Market Share–Customer Satisfaction Relationship," *Journal of Marketing* 77, no. 5 (September 1, 2013): 1–20, https://doi.org/10.1509/jm.09.0363. Claes Fornell, Forrest V. Morgeson III, and G. Tomas M. Hult, "Stock Returns on Customer Satisfaction Do Beat the Market: Gauging the Effect of a Marketing Intangible," *Journal of Marketing* 80, no. 5 (September 1, 2016): 92–107, https://doi.org/10.1509/jm.15.0229.

4. Frederick F. Reichheld, *The Loyalty Effect: The Hidden Force Behind Growth, Profits, and Lasting Value* (Boston: Harvard Business School Press, 1996), 50–51.

5. "About Us," *Mowi*, last modified June 27, 2024, https://mowi.com/about-us/.

6. Michael D. Johnson and Fred Selnes, "Customer Portfolio Management: Toward a Dynamic Theory of Exchange Relationships," *Journal of Marketing* 68, no. 2 (April 2004): 1–17, https://doi.org/10.1509/jmkg.68.2.1.27786. Michael D. Johnson and Fred Selnes, "Diversifying Your Customer Portfolio," *MIT Sloan Management Review* 46, no. 3 (April 1, 2005): 11–14. Selnes and Johnson, "Manage Your Customer Portfolio for Maximum Lifetime Value."

7. Michael E. Porter, *The Competitive Advantage: Creating and Sustaining Superior Performance* (New York: Free Press, 1985), 11–16.

8. Bo Edvardsson and Bo Enquist, "The IKEA Saga: How Service Culture Drives Strategy," *Service Industries Journal* 22, no. 4 (September 2002): 153–186.

Chapter 2

1. James R. Taylor, *Needs-Based Market Segmentation Strategies: How to Forecast Competitive Positions (and Make Millions)* (Ann Arbor, MI: Van Rye Publishing, 2022).

2. Peter Fader, *Customer Centricity: Focus on the Right Customers for Strategic Advantage* (Philadelphia: Wharton School Press, 2020).

3. Michael D. Johnson and Fred Selnes, "Customer Portfolio Management: Toward a Dynamic Theory of Exchange Relationships," *Journal of Marketing* 68, no. 2 (April 2004): 1–17, https://doi.org/10.1509/jmkg.68.2.1.27786.

4. Johnson and Selnes.

5. Fred Selnes and Michael D. Johnson, "Manage Your Customer Portfolio for Maximum Lifetime Value," *MIT Sloan Management Review* 64, no. 1 (2022): 22–27.

6. See, for example, Richard P. Bagozzi, "Marketing as Exchange," *Journal of Marketing* 39, no. 4 (October 1975): 32–39, https://doi.org/10.2307/1250593. Atul Parvatiyar and Jagdish N. Sheth, "The Domain and Conceptual Foundations of Relationship Marketing," in *Handbook of Relationship Marketing*, ed. Jagdish N. Sheth and Atul Parvatiyar (Thousand Oaks, CA: Sage, 2000), 3–38.

7. F. Robert Dwyer, Paul H. Schurr, and Sejo Oh, "Developing Buyer–Seller Relationships," *Journal of Marketing* 51, no. 2 (April 1987): 11–27, https://doi.org/10.2307/1251126.

8. Robert M. Morgan and Shelby D. Hunt, "The Commitment-Trust Theory of Relationship Marketing," *Journal of Marketing*, 58, no. 3 (July 1994): 20–38, https://doi.org/10.2307/1252308.

9. Barbara Bund Jackson, "Build Customer Relationships That Last," *Harvard Business Review* 63, no. 6 (November 1985): 120–128.

10. Jan B. Heide, "Interorganizational Governance in Marketing Channels," *Journal of Marketing* 58, no. 1 (January 1994): 71–85, https://doi.org/10.2307/1252252.

11. Erin Anderson and Barton Weitz, "The Use of Pledges to Build and Sustain Commitment in Distribution Channels," *Journal of Marketing Research* 29, no. 1 (February 1992): 18–34, https://doi.org/10.2307/3172490.

12. Kenneth H. Wathne, Jan B. Heide, Erik A. Mooi, and Alok Kumar, "Relationship Governance Dynamics: The Roles of Partner Selection Efforts and Mutual Investments," *Journal of Marketing Research* 55, no. 5 (October 2018): 704–721, https://www.jstor.org/stable/26966536. Oliver E. Williamson, "Transaction Cost Economics: The

Natural Progression," *American Economic Review* 100, no. 3 (June 2010): 673–690, https://doi.org/10.1257/aer.100.3.673.

13. Adapted from Johnson and Selnes "Customer Portfolio Management" and Selnes and Johnson "Manage Your Customer Portfolio for Maximum Lifetime Value."

14. See, for example, Barbara A. Gutek, *The Dynamics of Service: Reflections on the Changing Nature of Customer/Provider Interactions* (San Francisco: Jossey-Bass, 1995).

15. Our typology is similar to that in Krapfel, Salmond, and Spekman, but the definitions are different. See Robert E. Krapfel, Deborah Salmond, and Robert Spekman, "A Strategic Approach to Managing Buyer–Seller Relationships," *European Journal of Marketing* 25, no. 9 (September 1989): 22–37, https://doi.org/10.1108/EUM 0000000000622.

16. Marriott Bonvoy, *Marriott Bonvoy Elite*, revised November 2018, https://loyalty lobby.com/wp-content/uploads/2019/02/LL-Bonvoy-Benefits.pdf.

17. "Get to Know Medallion Status," *Delta Air Lines*, https://www.delta.com/us/en /skymiles/medallion-program/medallion-benefits.

18. Michael D. Johnson, Line Lervik-Olsen, and Tor Wallin Andreassen, "Joy and Disappointment in the Hotel Experience: Managing Relationship Segments," *Managing Service Quality* 19, no. 1 (January 2009): 4–30, https://doi.org/10.1108/096045 20910926782.

19. Anders Gustafsson, Michael D. Johnson, and Inger Roos, "The Effects of Customer Satisfaction, Relationship Commitment Dimensions, and Triggers on Customer Retention," *Journal of Marketing* 69, no. 4 (October 2005): 210–218, https:// doi.org/10.1509/jmkg.2005.69.4.210.

20. Albert M. Muniz Jr. and Thomas C. O'Guinn, "Brand Community," *Journal of Consumer Research* 27, no. 4 (March 2001): 412–432, https://doi.org/10.1086/319618.

21. James H. McAlexander, John W. Schouten, and Harold F. Koenig, "Building Brand Community," *Journal of Marketing* 66, no. 1 (January 2002): 38–54, https://doi .org/10.1509/jmkg.66.1.38.18451.

22. "Harley Owners Group Benefits," *Harley-Davidson*, https://www.harley-davidson .com/us/en/content/hog/membership-benefits.html.

23. "Harley to Highlight Custom Motorcycles," *Black Gold Harley-Davidson*, July 11, 2019, https://blackgoldhd.com/news-article/1075/harley-to-highlight-custom -motorcycles.

24. Andrew Cournoyer, "Harley-Davidson: Seeing Good Sales, but I Need More Proof to Believe the Tides Have Turned," *Seeking Alpha*, February 28, 2023, https:// seekingalpha.com/article/4582735-harley-davidson-seeing-good-sales-but-need -more-proof.

25. Michelle Watson, Cara Lynn Clarkson, and Ashley R. Williams, "Public Drunkenness, Disorderly Conduct Leads to 230 Arrests at Annual Texas Jeep Weekend Event," *CNN*, May 21, 2023, https://www.cnn.com/2023/05/21/us/texas-jeep-weekend-event-arrests/index.html.

26. See Stuart A. Bourdon, "What in the Duck is Jeep Ducking?" *MotorTrend*, March 4, 2024, https://www.motortrend.com/features/duck-duck-jeep/.

27. "Brand Ambassadors: Who Are They and What Do They Do?" *Radancy* (blog), October 12, 2022, https://blog.radancy.com/2022/10/12/brand-ambassadors-who-are-they-and-what-do-they-do/.

28. Susan Fournier, "Consumers and Their Brands: Developing Relationship Theory in Consumer Research," *Journal of Consumer Research* 24, no. 4 (March 1998): 343–353, https://doi.org/10.1086/209515.

29. Claudio Alvarez, Danielle J. Brick, and Susan Fournier (2021), "Doing Relationship Work: A Theory of Change in Consumer–Brand Relationships," *Journal of Consumer Research* 48, no. 4 (December 2021): 610–632, https://doi.org/10.1093/jcr/ucab022.

30. Peter Reid Dickson, "Toward a General Theory of Competitive Rationality," *Journal of Marketing* 56, no. 1 (January 1992): 69–83, https://doi.org/10.2307/1252133.

31. Calculated as the five-year discounted gross margin weighted by loyalty intention.

Chapter 3

1. Dave Chaffey, "Amazon.com Marketing Strategy 2023: E-commerce Retail Giant Business Case Study," *Smart Insights*, February 27, 2023, https://www.smartinsights.com/digital-marketing-strategy/online-business-revenue-models/amazon-case-study/.

2. Chaffey, "Amazon.com Marketing Strategy 2023."

3. "Awareness-Trial-Repeat (ATR)," *The Universal Marketing Dictionary*, https://marketing-dictionary.org/a/atr/.

4. Casey O'Connor, "Sales Funnel Management: Definition, Stages, & Tips," *Yesware*, March 9, 2022, https://www.yesware.com/blog/sales-funnel-management/.

5. Michael D. Johnson and Anders Gustafsson, *Improving Customer Satisfaction, Loyalty and Profit: An Integrated Measurement and Management System* (San Francisco: Jossey-Bass, 2000).

6. Chaffey, "Amazon.com Marketing Strategy 2023."

7. Mickey Toogood, "Amazon Selling Stats," *Amazon Grow Your Business* (blog), May 10, 2024, https://sell.amazon.com/blog/amazon-stats#:~:text=Amazon.com%20statistics&text=Amazon%20has%20over%20300%20million,1.9%20million%20selling%20partners%20worldwide.

8. Statista Research Department, "Annual Number of Worldwide Active Amazon Customer Accounts from 1997 to 2015," *Statista*, January 28, 2016, https://www.statista.com/statistics/237810/number-of-active-amazon-customer-accounts-worldwide/.

9. Albert Mosby, "Amazon Prime Statistics of 2024 (Users & Revenue)", February 21, 2024, https://www.yaguara.co/amazon-prime-statistics/#:~:text=There%20are%20230%20million%20Amazon,through%20Prime%20membership%20in%202023.

10. "Online Retailers: Reliable Benchmarks and Prescriptive Analytics to Help Online Retailers Improve Website Satisfaction," *American Customer Satisfaction Index*, last modified January 30, 2024, https://www.theacsi.org/industries/retail/online-retailers/.

11. "Amazon.com Announces Fourth Quarter Results," *Investor Relations: About Amazon*, February 1, 2024, https://ir.aboutamazon.com/news-release/news-release-details/2024/Amazon.com-Announces-Fourth-Quarter-Results/.

12. Jessica Lanman, "A Complete History of the iPod: From 2001 to 2022," *Make Use Of*, May 16, 2022, https://www.makeuseof.com/history-of-the-ipod/.

13. "Today at Apple," *Apple*, https://www.apple.com/today/.

14. Bo Edvardsson and Bo Enquist, "The IKEA Saga: How Service Culture Drives Strategy," Service Industries Journal, 22, no. 4 (September 2002), 153–186.

15. "Services," *IKEA*, https://www.ikea.com/us/en/customer-service/services/.

16. "IKEA Releases Sustainability Report FY21 and the First-Ever Climate Report, and Confirms Being on Track Towards 2030 Climate Commitment," *IKEA*, January 18, 2022, https://about.ikea.com/en/newsroom/2022/01/17/sustainability-report-fy21-and-climate-report.

17. "Norsk kundebarometer," *BI*, https://www.bi.no/forskning/norsk-kundebarometer/tidligere-resultater/.

18. Tomas Meehan, "If You Can't Beat 'em, Join 'em: How Nike Cornered the Running Shoe Market," *CNN*, May 18, 2021, https://www.cnn.com/2021/05/18/sport/nike-running-shoes-spt-intl-cmd/index.html.

19. "Our Brand Icon," *Scottish Widows*, https://www.scottishwidows.co.uk/about-us/who-we-are/our-brand.html.

20. "Ontex Develops New Smart Diaper Solution for Incontinence," *Ontex*, February 18, 2021, https://ontex.com/news/brands/ontex-develops-new-smart-diaper-solution-for-incontinence/.

21. OneCall, https://www.onecallsim.com/.

22. "Sector Alarm at a Glance," *Sector Alarm*, https://www.sectoralarm.com/about-us/.

23. "Top 12 Reasons Students Transfer Colleges," *Best Colleges*, March 21, 2023, https://www.bestcolleges.com/blog/top-reasons-students-transfer-colleges/.

24. "About SATS," *SATS*, https://satsgroup.com/about-sats/.

25. Fred Selnes and Michael D. Johnson, "Manage Your Customer Portfolio for Maximum Lifetime Value," *MIT Sloan Management Review* 64, no. 1 (2022): 23.

Chapter 4

1. Claes Fornell and Birger Wernerfelt, "Defensive Marketing Strategy by Customer Complaint Management: A Theoretical Analysis," *Journal of Marketing Research* 24, no. 4 (November 1987): 337–346, https://doi.org/10.2307/3151381. See also Michael D. Johnson, *Customer Orientation and Market Action* (Upper Saddle River, NJ: Prentice Hall, 1998), 46.

2. See John A. Howard, "Foundations of Consumer Behavior," chap. 2 in *Consumer Behavior in Marketing Strategy* (Englewood Cliffs, NJ: Prentice Hall, 1989), 11–26.

3. An earlier version of the model was published in Michael D. Johnson and Fred Selnes, "Customer Portfolio Management: Toward a Dynamic Theory of Exchange Relationships," *Journal of Marketing* 68, no. 2 (April 2004): 1–17, https://doi.org/10.1509/jmkg.68.2.1.27786. In the new model we introduced brand extension to investigate the dynamics of CPLV under different conditions of market heterogeneity. We also extended the analysis to investigate the effects when a company invests disproportionately in offensive, defensive, and relationship conversion strategies. The basic structure of the model is as before, but we adjusted the specific parameters related to customer behavior and response elasticities to different strategies.

4. Michael E. Porter, "Competitive Strategy–The Core Concepts," chap. 1 in *Competitive Advantage: Creating and Sustaining Superior Performance* (New York: Free Press, 1985), 1–30.

5. Roger L. Martin, "The Age of Customer Capitalism," *Harvard Business Review* 88, no. 1 (January–February 2010): 58–65.

6. Claes Fornell, "A National Customer Satisfaction Barometer: The Swedish Experience," *Journal of Marketing* 56, no. 1 (January 1992): 6–21, https://doi.org/10.2307/1252129. See also Michael D. Johnson, *Customer Orientation and Market Action* (Upper Saddle River, NJ: Prentice Hall, 1998), 42.

7. For an excellent discussion of competition and market dynamics, see Peter Reid Dickson, "Toward a General Theory of Competitive Rationality," *Journal of Marketing* 56, no. 1 (January 1992): 69–83, https://doi.org/10.2307/1252133.

8. This argument is consistent with the resource-based view on strategy as originally suggested by Jay Barney, "Firm Resources and Sustained Competitive Advantage,"

Journal of Management 17, no. 1 (March 1991): 99–120, https://doi.org/10.1177 /014920639101700108. The argument is also consistent with Michael Porter's idea of a "system of linked activities," as presented in Michael E. Porter, "What Is Strategy?" *Harvard Business Review* 74, no. 6 (November–December 1996): 59–79.

9. See for example Franziska Völckner and Henrik Sattler, "Drivers of Brand Extension Success," *Journal of Marketing* 70, no. 2 (April 2006): 18–34, https://doi.org /10.1509/jmkg.70.2.018.

10. Johnson and Selnes, "Customer Portfolio Management."

Chapter 5

1. Ajay K. Kohli and Bernard J. Jaworski (1990), "Market Orientation: The Construct, Research Propositions, and Managerial Implications," *Journal of Marketing* 54, no. 2 (April 1990): 1–18, https://doi.org/10.2307/1251866.

2. Claes Fornell, Michael D. Johnson, Eugene W. Anderson, Jaesung Cha, and Barbara Everitt Bryant, "The American Customer Satisfaction Index: Nature, Purpose, and Findings," *Journal of Marketing* 60, no. 4 (October 1996): 7–18, https://doi.org /10.2307/1251898.

3. The analysts applied a nonnegative matrix factorization (NMF) method which has become a widely used tool for the analysis of high-dimensional data with many zeros in the dataset. The method automatically extracts sparse and meaningful features from a set of nonnegative data vectors.

4. Fornell et al., "The American Customer Satisfaction Index."

5. Maximilian Richter, Nikolaus Lang, Markus Hagenmaier, Andreas Herrmann, and Michael D. Johnson, "Whose Disruptions are Winning the Autonomous Driving Race? When Disruptive Innovations Come to Cities," *California Management Review*, June 13, 2022, https://cmr.berkeley.edu/2022/06/whose-disruptions-are-winning-the -autonomous-driving-race/.

6. For a technical note on comparing groups in field experiments, see Alberto Abadie, Alexis Diamond, and Jens Hainmueller, "Comparative Politics and the Synthetic Control Method," *American Journal of Political Science* 59, no. 2 (April 2015): 495–510, https://doi.org/10.1111/ajps.12116.

7. John Stuart Mill, "A System of Logic, Ratiocinative and Inductive, being a Connected View of the Principles of Evidence, and the Methods of Scientific Investigation," 3rd ed., *North American Review* 78, no. 162 (January 1854): 82–105.

8. Michael D. Johnson and Anders Gustafsson, *Improving Customer Satisfaction, Loyalty and Profit: An Integrated Measurement and Management System* (San Francisco: Jossey-Bass, 2000).

9. R. M. Baron and D. A. Kenny, "The Moderator–Mediator Variable Distinction in Social Psychological Research: Conceptual, Strategic, and Statistical Considerations," *Journal of Personality and Social Psychology* 51, no. 6 (1986): 1173–1182, https://doi .org/10.1037/0022-3514.51.6.1173.

10. Michael D. Johnson, Andreas Herrmann, and Frank Huber, "The Evolution of Loyalty Intentions," *Journal of Marketing* 70, no. 2 (April 2006): 122–132, https://doi .org/10.1509/jmkg.70.2.122.

11. Lyle Yorks, "Nothing So Practical as a Good Theory," *Human Resource Development Review* 4, no. 2 (June 2005): 111–113, https://doi.org/10.1177/1534484305276176.

12. Galit Shmueli, "To Explain or to Predict?" *Statistical Science* 25, no. 3 (August 2010): 289–310, https://doi.org/10.1214/10-STS330.

13. See Brett Lantz, *Machine Learning with R*, 4th ed. (Birmingham, UK: Packt, 2023) for an excellent introduction to machine learning. The book provides an overview of the many methods that are now available and used in machine learning.

Chapter 6

1. "Common Pitfalls of Customer Experience Measurement (and How to Avoid Them)," *Hanover Research*, January 9, 2017, https://www.hanoverresearch.com/reports -and-briefs/common-pitfalls-customer-experience-measurement/?org=corporate.

2. Michael D. Johnson, "Customer Satisfaction," in *International Encyclopedia of the Social & Behavioral Sciences*, ed. Neil J. Smelser and Paul B. Baltes, vol. 5 (Oxford: Pergamon, 2001), 3198–3202, https://doi.org/10.1016/B0-08-043076-7/04273-X.

3. Anders Gustafsson and Michael D. Johnson, *Competing in a Service Economy: How to Create a Competitive Advantage Through Service Development and Innovation* (San Francisco: Jossey-Bass, 2003), 16, 33. See also Jan Carlzon, *Moments of Truth: New Strategies for Today's Customer-Driven Economy* (New York: Harper & Row, 1987).

4. Claes Fornell, Michael D. Johnson, Eugene W. Anderson, Jaesung Cha, and Barbara Everitt Bryant, "The American Customer Satisfaction Index: Nature, Purpose, and Findings," *Journal of Marketing* 60, no. 4 (October 1996): 7–18, https://doi.org/10 .2307/1251898.

5. Michael D. Johnson and Anders Gustafsson, *Improving Customer Satisfaction, Loyalty and Profit: An Integrated Measurement and Management System* (San Francisco: Jossey-Bass, 2000).

6. This example is based on two 2022 case studies by Michael D. Johnson, "Badger Tire Company A Case: Building the Lens of the Customer" and "Badger Tire Company B Case: Priority Setting Using Impact-Performance Analysis." Both case studies are available directly from the author (mdj27@cornell.edu).

7. For a detailed description of the CIT method see Bob E. Hayes, *Measuring Customer Satisfaction: Survey Design, Use, and Statistical Analysis Method* (Milwaukee, WI: American Society for Quality, 1998) 16–18.

8. Gustafsson and Johnson, *Competing in a Service Economy*, 133–137.

9. Anders Gustafsson and Michael D. Johnson, "Determining Attribute Importance in a Service Satisfaction Model," *Journal of Service Research* 7, no. 2 (November 2004): 124–141, https://doi.org/10.1177/1094670504268453.

Chapter 7

1. "'Half the money I spend on advertising is wasted; the trouble is I don't know which half.' | B2B Marketing," *B2B Marketing*, last modified April 2, 2024, https://www.b2bmarketing.net/archive/half-the-money-i-spend-on-advertising-is-wasted-the-trouble-is-i-dont-know-which-half-b2b-marketing/.

2. Peter Fader, *Customer Centricity: Focus on the Right Customers for Strategic Advantage* (Philadelphia: Wharton School Press, 2020).

3. Roger L. Martin, "The Age of Customer Capitalism," *Harvard Business Review* 88, no. 1 (January–February 2010): 58–65.

4. Theodore Levitt, "Marketing Myopia," repr. *Harvard Business Review* 53, no. 5 (September–October 1975).

5. Marriott International, *Marriott International 2020 Annual Report*, February 18, 2021, https://marriott.gcs-web.com/static-files/c5e1faef-f1e5-40e3-bd70-5efbbb929a7f.

6. Peter F. Drucker, *The Practice of Management* (New York: Harper & Row, 1954), 416.

7. Ajay K. Kohli and Bernard J. Jaworski, "Market Orientation: The Construct, Research Propositions, and Managerial Implications," *Journal of Marketing* 54, no. 2 (April 1990): 1–18, https://doi.org/10.2307/1251866.

8. John C. Narver and Stanley F. Slater, "The Effect of a Market Orientation on Business Profitability," *Journal of Marketing* 54, no. 4 (October 1990): 20–35, https://doi.org/10.2307/1251757.

9. Fred Selnes and Even J. Lanseng, *Marketing Management: A Customer-Centric Approach* (Thousand Oaks, CA: Sage, forthcoming).

10. Anders Gustafsson and Michael D. Johnson, "Bridging the Quality-Satisfaction Gap," *Quality Management Journal* 4, no. 3 (April 1997): 27–43, https://doi.org/10.1080/10686967.1997.11918801.

11. Eugene W. Anderson, Claes Fornell, and Donald R. Lehmann, "Customer Satisfaction, Market Share, and Profitability: Findings from Sweden," *Journal of Marketing* 58, no. 3 (July 1994): 53–66, https://doi.org/10.2307/1252310.

12. Lopo L. Rego, Neil A. Morgan, and Claes Fornell, "Reexamining the Market Share–Customer Satisfaction Relationship," *Journal of Marketing* 77, no. 5 (September 2013): 1–20, https://doi.org/10.1509/jm.09.0363.

13. Peter Economy, "17 Powerfully Inspiring Quotes from Southwest Airlines Founder Herb Kelleher," *Inc.*, January 4, 2019, https://www.inc.com/peter-economy /17-powerfully-inspiring-quotes-from-southwest-airlines-founder-herb-kelleher.html.

Chapter 8

1. Michael L. Katz and Carl Shapiro, "Technology Adoption in the Presence of Network Externalities," *Journal of Political Economy* 94, no. 4 (June 1985): 822–841; Brian Uzzi, "The Sources and Consequences of Embeddedness for the Economic Performance of Organizations: The Network Effect," *American Sociological Review* 61, no. 4 (August 1996): 674–698.

2. Raji Srinivasan, Gary L. Lilien and Arvind Rangaswamy, "First In, First Out? The Effects of Network Externalities on Pioneer Survival," *Journal of Marketing* 68, no. 1 (January 2004): 41–58.

3. See, for example: Lauren Thomas, "Choice Hotels Launches Hostile Bid for Wyndham," *Wall Street Journal*, December 12, 2023, https://www.wsj.com/business/deals /choice-hotels-launches-hostile-bid-for-wyndham-c31d1230.

4. Allison Pohle, "Why Doesn't Airbnb Have a Loyalty Program Like Everyone Else?" *Wall Street Journal*, July 19, 2023, https://www.wsj.com/articles/airbnb-vrbo-loyalty -program-c72306f.

Index

Note: Page numbers in italics denote references to figures.

A/B testing, 73
AC Hotels, 102
Acquaintances
  building materials retailer example and, 23–24
  cash flow and, 51, 52, *53*
  converting to friends, 35, 55
  customer heterogeneity and, 49
  defending, 38–39
  description of, 15–16
  leveraging, 41
  market shocks and, 58–59
  Pan Fish example and, 3
  segmentation and, 7, 9, 10, 108
  strategies and action steps for, *43*
  value propositions of, 14, *14*
Add-on services, 41
Advertising, innovative, 34–35. *See also* Marketing strategies
Airbnb, 22, 112
Algorithms, published, 80
Altibox, 34
Amazon, 7, 15, 28–30, 37, 42, 45, 52, 84, 99–100, 110, 111, 113
Amazon Prime, 30, 111
American Customer Satisfaction Index, 2, 67, 70
American Institute of Public Opinion, 70

Analytics, 7
Apple, 7, 15, 30–31, 42, 45
Apple TV+, 31
Artificial intelligence (AI), 107
Averages, 72–73
Awareness-trial-repeat (ATR), 29, 33

B2B (business-to-business) firms, 3, 6, 13, 17, 36
B2C (business-to-consumer) companies, 6, 18–20
Beta coefficients, 68
Bezos, Jeff, 28, 113
Brand adaptation, 40
Brand ambassadors, 20, 45
Brand awareness, 33, 35, 38, *43*, 44, 99
Brand communities, 6, 18–20, 42, 44
Brand differentiation, 12
Brand extension strategies, 48, 57–58
Brand management, 102–103, *103*
Brand–relationship matrix, 103–104
Brands, portfolio of, 9–10
Brand-value propositions, 104
Building materials retailer example, 23–25, 66, 108
Bulgari, 102
Business performance
  impacts on, 92–94
  linking CPM strategies to, 83–95

Business performance (cont.)
   linking quality and satisfaction to,
     86–87

Cash flow, estimating, 21, 51–52, *53*
Categorizations, 65
Causal mechanisms/causality, 7, 63, *64*,
   75–79, 110
Central tendency, measures of, 74
Churn. *See also* Relationships: defense
   of; Retention
   defensive marketing strategies and,
     54
   loyalty and, 37–38
   management of, 37
   predicting, 18
   protecting from, 12, 27
Competitive advantages, 94–95, 109
Competitive disadvantages, 95
Competitor data, 68, 71
Competitors, acquiring customers from,
   33–34, 54
Constructed market, 48–52
Contract renewals, 37
Contractual relationships, 37, 40–41
Contribution margin, 49
Conversion strategies, 59–60, *60*, 61
Costco, 41
Cost leadership, 13, 42, 111
Courtyard by Marriott, 102
CPM analytics
   basic workflows for, 63–64, *64*
   causality and, 75–79
   descriptive statistics and, 64–75
   predictive score modeling and, 79–81
CPM roadmap, 107–114
CPM strategies
   at IKEA, 32–33
   linking to business performance,
     83–95
   review of, 107–110
Critical incident technique, 88
Cross-selling, 40–41, 45, 58, 111

Cumulative (cross-transactional)
   customer satisfaction, 84–85, 94
Customer acquisition
   Amazon and, 29
   customer heterogeneity and, 57
   framework and, 7, 9, *10*
   investments in, 12, 27
   ongoing, 5
   relationship conversion and, 14,
     33–35
   simulating, 54–57, *56*
   strategies and action steps for, *43*, 44
Customer-centric focus, 28
Customer centricity, 97–98
Customer database and measurement
   systems, 28, 63, 64–75, 110
Customer evaluations, 85
Customer heterogeneity, 47–49, *50*, 52,
   53, 55–61, *56*, 109
Customer journey mapping, 69, 84–85
Customer lifetime value (CLV), 10–11,
   12, 23–24
Customer portfolio lifetime value
   (CPLV)
   constructed market and, 48–52
   framework and, 9, 10–12
   model for, 47–48, 60–61
   prescriptive strategies and, 52–60
   relationship trajectories and, 21
   scale economies and, 8
Customer portfolio management, 102–
   103, *103*
Customer relationship management
   (CRM), 12–13
Customer satisfaction
   CPM analytics and, 63–64
   defending acquaintances and, 38
   defense and, 57
   importance of, 2–3
   market share versus, 104–106
   measuring, 84–85
   model of, 7, 86–87, *86*, 94
   as offensive strategy, 54

optimizing, 92
as priority, 52
quality and, 76–77
quality and cost and, 110
survey of, 67
transactional versus cumulative, 84–85
variability and, 72–73
visit frequency and, 71
Customer survey data, 68, 70–71
Customer-to-customer relationships, 42
Customer trajectories, 20–23
Customization, 7, 30–33, 36, 44, 47–48, 55

Data analytics, 29
Database principles, 7
Data quality and control, 64, 74–75
Data quality management, 74–75
Data sources, integrating, 64, 68–72
Data streams, continuous, 64
Defections, 12
Defensive strategies, 7, 29, 47, 52, 54–61, 56, 60, 104, 106, 109
Demographic information, 71
Descriptive statistics, 7, 63, 64–75, 64
Differentiation, 7, 13, 30–33, 34, 42, 44, 45, 47–48, 55, 111
Diffusion pattern, 33
Digital communication channels, 41
Digitalization, 7, 36–37, 107, 111–112
Digital marketing strategies, 28–29
Disney, 84
Dispersion, measures of, 74
Dissatisfaction, 34, 38–39, 55. See also Customer satisfaction
Diversification, 30
Drucker, Peter, 102

Economies of scale and scope, 47, 61, 110–111
Educational institutions, 39–40

Email marketing, 99–100
Encounters, 16
Estranged customers. See Strangers
Exchange relationships, 13
Experimentation, 73

First-mover advantage, 111
Fitness centers, 41
Follower strategies, 56, 56, 59–60, 60
Friends
building materials retailer example and, 23–24
cash flow and, 52, 53
converting acquaintances to, 35
converting to partners, 35–37, 55
defending, 39–40
description of, 15–16
leveraging, 41–42
Pan Fish example and, 3
partners versus, 13
segmentation and, 7, 9, 10, 108
strategies and action steps for, 43
value propositions of, 14, 14

Gallup, George, 70
Gallup, Inc., 70
Goal setting, 109–110
Growth strategies, 7

Harley-Davidson, 19
Harley HOGS, 19
Heterogeneity, 21–23, 47
High investment strategies, 55–56, 56
Hilton, 112
House of quality, 104

iCloud data storage, 31
IKEA, 6, 7, 30–33, 41, 45
Impact-performance analysis, 87–89, 90, 91–92, 110
Industrial marketing, 13
Influencers, 20
Innovation, 34

Interaction data, 68, 69–70
Interactions, effect of, 18
Investments in acquisition, 55–56
iPhone, 31
iPod, 31
iTunes Store, 31

Jeep, 19–20
Journey maps, 69, 84–85

Kamprad, Ingvar, 31–32
Kelleher, Herb, 106
Key business performance indicators
    (KPIs), 75, 98

"Leaky bucket" model, 2, 4–6
Learning curve effects, 47
Levitt, Ted, 101
Lewin, Kurt, 78
Location data, 68, 70–71
Loyalty
    churn and, 37–38
    effect of, 2–3
    fleeting nature of, 5
    impact of quality and price on, 77
    increasing, 12
    lifetime value and, 8
Loyalty programs, 17, 22, 36, 41, 55,
    103, 112

Machine learning, 80, 107
macOS, 111
Macrosegments, 101–102, 103–104,
    105
Management decisions, 7, 12
Marketing function, 99–100
Marketing management, 7, 14, 101–
    102
"Marketing Myopia" (Levitt), 101
Marketing strategies, offensive versus
    defensive, 7, 29, 47, 52, 54, 59–60,
    60, 104, 106, 109
Market matrix, 102–104

Market orientation, 63
Market share
    customer satisfaction versus, 104–106
    gains in, 104–105
Market shocks, 58–60, 61
Marriott, 101–102, 103, 112, 113
Marriott Bonvoy, 17, 21, 103
Martin, Roger, 52
Mediation, testing for, 76–77, 76
Mergers and acquisitions (M&A), 112
Microsegments, 101, 104, 105
Mill, John Stuart, 75
Mobile apps, 36–37, 55
Mobility data, 72
Mowi ASA, 3

Net promoter scores, 93
Nike, 34, 45, 78
Noncontractual relationships, 37, 40,
    41

Offensive strategies, 7, 29, 47, 52, 54,
    59–61, 60, 104, 106, 109
OneCall, 38
Ontex, 37
Output, interpreting, 89, 91–92

Pan Fish, 3, 10, 13, 17, 36, 45, 113
Partner networks, 112
Partners
    building materials retailer example
        and, 23–24
    cash flow and, 52, 53
    converting friends to, 35
    defending, 40
    description of, 15–16
    friends versus, 13
    leveraging, 42
    Pan Fish example and, 3
    segmentation and, 7, 9, 10, 108
    strategies and action steps for, 43
    sunsetting, 44–45
    value propositions of, 14, 14

Partnerships, 6
Personal selling, 100
Porter, Michael, 4, 42, 52
Predictive score modeling, 64, *64*, 70, 79–81, 110
Predictive scoring analytics, 7
Predictors, 66–67, 69
Preorder processes, 36, 55
Prescriptive strategies, 52–60
Procter & Gamble, 52, 101
Product differentiation, 30, 45
Product diffusion models, 29
Product innovation, 34
Product portfolio management, 102–103, *103*
Product quality, 86–87, *86*
Program differentiation, 31
Pseudo-relationships, 16

Qualitative interviews, 88–89
Quality, 86–87
Quality, perceived, 67, 76–77
Quality function deployment (QFD), 104

Recommendation systems, 37
Regression models, 68, 76–77, *76*, *78*
REI, 41
Relationship expectations, 40
Relationships
    allocation and, 65–66
    conversion of, 7, 9, 12, 14, 21, 27, 30, 35–37, *43*, 54–57, *56*
    customer-to-customer, 42
    defense of, 7, 9, 12, 27, 30, 37–40, *43*, 44, 54–57, *56*
    exchange, 13
    investments in, 48
    leverage of, 7, 9, 11, 12, 27, 30, 40–42, *43*, 57–58
    return on investment in, 4
    value of, 2–4
Retail applications, 23–25

Retention, 7, 18, 44, 49, 54–55, 58, 76–77. *See also* Churn
RevPAR (revenue per available room), 92–93
Ritz-Carlton, 102
Roadmap
    CPM, 107–114
    developing, 112–113

Sales, focus on, 2
SAS, 84
Satisfaction models, 76–77, 99. *See also* Customer satisfaction
SATS, 41
Scale economies, 8, 47–48
Scottish Widows, 34–35, 45, 78
Search histories, 29
Seasonality, 78, *78*
Sector Alarm, 38–39, 45, 100, 113
Segmentation
    market, 9
    needs-based, 9, 12, 35, 101–102, 103, 106
    relationship, 3, 6, 7, 9, 10, 11–12, 13–16, 64, 107–110
Self-rated importance measures, 93
Service differentiation, 30–31
Service quality, 86–87, *86*
Shared costs, 11
Shareholder value, 52
Six Sigma, 87
SkyMiles, 17
Smart variables, 64, 65–68
Southwest Airlines, 106
Spotify, 37
S-shaped diffusion curve, 33, 48, 51
Starbucks, 36–37, 55
Strangers
    converting to acquaintances, 16
    customer acquisition and, 33
    defending, 38
    knowledgeable, 44
    segmentation and, 7, 9, 10, 108

Strangers (cont.)
strategies and action steps for, *43*
value of, 11
value propositions of, 14, *14*
Strategies and action steps, CPM guide
to, 42–45
Sunsetting partners, 44–45
Sustainability, 32
Switching barriers, 37, 54
Switching costs, 13, 18, 40, 48, 111–112

TaskRabbit, 32
Tesla, 19, 22–23
Tire company application, 87–89, *90*,
91–92
Today at Apple, 31
Top-box scores, 93
Top management, importance of
involvement of, 98–99, 108, 113
Touchpoints, 84
Transactional data, 65, 68–69
Transactional expectations, 40
Transaction-specific satisfaction, 84–
85, 94
Trust, 34–35
TUI fly Nordic, 41–42, 45

Uncertainty, reducing, 69

Value, capturing, 97–106
Value-added services, 35, 45
Value/price, 86–87, *86*
Variability, embracing, 64, 72–74
Variables, constructing smart, 64, 65–68

Wanamaker, John, 97
Win-back programs, 66
Windows, 111